ExpressWays

ENGLISH FOR COMMUNICATION

1B

Steven J. Molinsky · Bill Bliss

 PRENTICE HALL REGENTS, Englewood Cliffs, NJ 07632

Library of Congress Cataloging-in-Publication Data
(Revised for vol. 1)

Molinsky, Steven J.
  ExpressWays : English for communication.

  Includes indexes.
  1. English language—Text-books for foreign speakers.
I. Bliss, Bill.   II. Title.
PE1128.M674   1986   428.3'4   85-30059
ISBN 0-13-298423-7 (v. 1)

Editorial/production supervision and
  interior design: Sylvia Moore
Development: Ellen Lehrburger
Cover design: Lundgren Graphics, Ltd.
Manufacturing buyer: Lorraine Fumoso
Page layout: Diane Koromhas

Illustrations and cover drawing by Gabriel Polonsky

Printed in the United States of America

10   9   8

ISBN   0-13-298449-0

Prentice-Hall International (UK) Limited, *London*
Prentice-Hall of Australia Pty. Limited, *Sydney*
Prentice-Hall Canada Inc., *Toronto*
Prentice-Hall Hispanoamericana, S.A., *Mexico*
Prentice-Hall of India Private Limited, *New Delhi*
Prentice-Hall of Japan, Inc., *Tokyo*
Prentice-Hall of Southeast Asia Pte. Ltd., *Singapore*
Editora Prentice-Hall do Brasil, Ltda., *Rio de Janeiro*

Contents

Asking for and Reporting Information • Instructing • Identifying
• Requests • Checking and Indicating Understanding
• Asking for Repetition • Initiating Conversations

FOOD • SUPERMARKET • RESTAURANT AND FOOD SERVICES • MONEY

Partitives • Would • Count/Non-Count Nouns
• Imperatives • May • Adjectives

Want-Desire • Complimenting • Requests • Preference
• Instructing • Persuading-Insisting
• Checking and Indicating Understanding • Hesitating

FINANCES • MONEY • BANKING • HOUSING

Adjectives • Comparatives • Superlatives
• Ordinal Numbers • Past Tense • Should
• Future: Going to • Have to • Time Expressions
• Imperatives • This/That

Remembering/Forgetting • Describing • Agreement/Disagreement
• Certainty/Uncertainty • Advice-Suggestions
• Checking and Indicating Understanding • Initiating a Topic

EMPLOYMENT/ON THE JOB

Adjectives • Adverbs • Comparative of Adverbs
• Reflexive Pronouns • Past Tense • Imperatives
• Present Continuous Tense • Future: Will
• Time Expressions • Supposed to • Have Got to
• Might • Should • Two-Word Verbs

Correcting • Approval/Disapproval • Obligation • Warning
• Advice-Suggestions • Complimenting • Promising
• Checking and Indicating Understanding • Asking for Repetition

APPENDIX

INDEXES

TO THE TEACHER

ExpressWays is a functional English program for adult and young-adult learners of English. The program consists of the following components:

Student Course Books—offering intensive conversational practice;
Companion Workbooks—offering grammar, reading, writing, and listening comprehension practice fully coordinated with the student course books;
Guide Books—providing background notes and expansion activities for all lessons and step-by-step instructions for teachers;
Audio Program—offering realistic presentation of dialogs in the texts;
Picture Program—including Picture Cards for vocabulary development and Dialog Visual Cards that depict scenes and characters from the texts;
Placement and Achievement Testing Program—providing tools for the evaluation of student levels and progress.

ExpressWays—Book 1 is intended for adult and young-adult students of English at the beginning level. The text provides an introduction to basic grammar and vocabulary and the usage of English for everyday life situations. *ExpressWays—Book 1* is organized by topics, or competencies, while incorporating integrated coverage of functions and beginning-level grammar.*

THE DIMENSIONS OF COMMUNICATION: FUNCTION, FORM, AND CONTENT

A number of texts present a "topical," or competency-based, syllabus by covering vocabulary items and key expressions needed for specific situations. A number of other texts present a "functional" syllabus by describing language use and listing sets of functional phrases. In both cases, texts tend to focus exclusively on the one dimension of communication that organizes the syllabus. In addition, both topical and functional texts do not usually give students intensive communicative practice using the correct grammatical forms that are required by particular key expressions or functional language choices.

---

* *ExpressWays—Books 1 and 2* are organized by a spiralled curriculum. They are based on a core topical curriculum that is covered at different degrees of intensity and depth at each level. *ExpressWays—Book 1* provides students with the most important vocabulary, grammar, and functional expressions needed to communicate at a basic level in a full range of situations and contexts. *ExpressWays—Book 2* covers the same full range of situations and contexts, but offers students expanded vocabulary, more complex grammar, and a wider choice of functional expressions.

ExpressWays—Book 3 is organized by functions, while incorporating integrated coverage of higher level topics and grammar. *ExpressWays—Foundations* is a simplified edition of Book 1, for students who require more basic material and who perhaps have more limited reading and writing skills.

ExpressWays—Book 1 aims to provide dynamic, communicative practice that involves students in lively interactions based on the content of real-life contexts and situations. The topically organized syllabus is fully integrated into a complete conversational course in which students not only learn the vocabulary and expressions needed for essential life situations, but also learn the various ways to express the functions of English and intensively practice the grammatical forms required to competently produce these expressions and functions.

Every lesson in the program offers students simultaneous practice with one or more functions, the grammatical forms needed to express those functions, and the contexts and situations in which the functions and grammar are used. This "tri-dimensional clustering" of function, form, and content is the organizing principle behind each lesson and the cornerstone of the *ExpressWays* approach to functional syllabus design.

ExpressWays aims to offer students broad exposure to uses of language in a variety of relevant contexts: in community, academic, employment, home, and social settings. The characters portrayed are people of different ages, ethnic groups, and occupations, interacting in real-life situations.

While some texts make a point of giving students a range of ways of expressing a function, from extremely polite to very impolite, we have chosen to "take the middle ground" and concentrate on those expressions that would most frequently occur in normal polite conversation between people in various settings. *ExpressWays* does offer a variety of registers, from the formal language someone might use in a job interview, with a customer, or when speaking with an authority figure, to the informal language someone would use when talking with family members, co-workers, or friends.

A special feature of the program is the treatment of discourse strategies. Students actively practice initiating conversations and topics, hesitating, checking and indicating understanding, and other conversation skills.

AN OVERVIEW

Guided Conversations

Guided Conversations are the dialogs and exercises that are the central learning devices in the program. Each lesson begins with a model guided conversation that depicts a real-life situation and the vocabulary, grammar, and functions used in the communication exchange. In the exercises that follow, students create new conversations by placing new contexts, content, or characters into the framework of the model.

"Now Present Your Own Conversations"

Each lesson ends with this open-ended exercise which offers students the opportunity to create and present original conversations based on the model. Students contribute content based on their experiences, ideas, and imaginations, while staying within the framework of the model.

We should emphasize that the objective of each lesson is to provide a measure of controlled practice with a dialog and guided conversation exercises so that students can competently create their own, original conversations.

Interchange

This end-of-chapter activity offers students the opportunity to create and present "guided role plays." Each activity consists of a model that students can practice and then use as a basis for their original presentations. Students should be encouraged to be inventive and to use new vocabulary in these presentations and should feel free to adapt and expand the model any way they wish.

Scenes & Improvisations

These "free role plays" appear after every third chapter, offering review and synthesis of lessons in the three preceding chapters. Students are presented with eight scenes depicting conversations between people in various situations. They use the information in the scenes to determine who the people are and what they are talking about. Then, students improvise based on their perceptions of the scenes' characters, contexts, and situations.

The purpose of these improvisations is to offer free recombination practice that promotes students' absorption of the preceding chapters' vocabulary, grammar, and functions into their repertoire of active language use.

Support and Reference Sections

ExpressWays offers a number of support and reference sections:

- *Chapter Opening Pages* provide an overview of topics, grammar, and key functions and conversation strategies highlighted in each chapter.
- *End-of-Chapter Summaries* provide complete lists of topic vocabulary and grammar structures appearing in each chapter.
- A *Chapter-by-Chapter Summary of Functions and Conversation Strategies* in the Appendix provides an overview of all expressions for the functions and conversation strategies in each chapter.
- A *Topic Vocabulary Glossary* provides a listing of key vocabulary domains included in the text and indicates the pages where the words first appear.
- An *Index of Functions and Conversation Strategies*, an *Index of Topics* and an *Index of Grammatical Structures* provide a convenient reference for locating coverage of functions, topics, and grammar in the text.

THE TOTAL *ExpressWays* PROGRAM

The *ExpressWays Student Course Books* are essentially designed to offer intensive communicative practice. These texts may be used independently, or in conjunction with the *ExpressWays Companion Workbooks*, which offer practice in the other skill areas of reading, writing, and listening, as well as focused practice with particular grammar structures as they occur in the program. Each exercise in the Companion Workbook indicates the specific Student Course Book page that it corresponds to.

The *ExpressWays Guide Books* provide step-by-step instructions for coverage of each lesson, background notes, sample answers to guided conversation exercises, and answer keys and listening-activity scripts for exercises in the Companion Workbooks. For teachers of multi-level classes, the Guide Books indicate for each lesson the corresponding page in *ExpressWays—Foundations* that covers the same topic at a lower level, and the corresponding page in *ExpressWays—Book 2* that covers the same topic at a higher level.

Perhaps the most important feature of the Guide Books is the expansion exercise that is recommended for each lesson. These exercises offer students free, spontaneous practice with the vocabulary, grammar, and functions that are presented in the Student Course Books. Activities include improvisations, "information gap" role plays, problem-solving, and topics for discussion and debate. We encourage teachers to use these activities or similar ones as springboards to help their students "break away" from the text and incorporate lesson content into their everyday use of English.

The *ExpressWays Audio Program* includes a set of tapes providing realistic presentation of all model dialogs and selected guided conversation exercises in the Student Course Books. The tapes are designed to be used interactively, so that the recorded voice serves as the student's speaking partner, making conversation practice possible even when the student is studying alone. The Audio Program also includes a set of tapes for the listening comprehension exercises in the Companion Workbooks.

The *ExpressWays Picture Program* includes Dialog Visual Cards and Picture Cards. The *ExpressWays Dialog Visual Cards* are poster-size illustrations depicting the characters and settings of all model dialogs. Their use during introduction of the model helps to assure that students are engaged in active listening and speaking practice during this important stage in the lesson. The *ExpressWays Picture Cards* illustrate key concepts and vocabulary items. They can be used for introduction of new material, for review, for enrichment exercises, and for role-playing activities.

The *ExpressWays Testing Program* includes a Placement Testing Kit for initial evaluation and leveling of students, and sets of Mid-Term and Final Examinations to measure students' achievement at each level of the program. All tests in the program include both oral and written evaluation components.

SUGGESTED TEACHING STRATEGIES

In using *ExpressWays*, we encourage you to develop approaches and strategies that are compatible with your own teaching style and the needs and abilities of your students. While the program does not require any specific method or technique in order to be used effectively, you may find it helpful to review and try out some of the following suggestions. (Specific step-by-step instructions may be found in the Guide Books.)

Guided Conversations

1. *Setting the Scene.* Have students look at the model illustration in the book or on the *ExpressWays* Dialog Visual Card. Set the scene: Who are the people? What is the situation?
2. *Listening to the Model.* With books closed, have students listen to the model conversation—presented by you, a pair of students, or on the audio tape.
3. *Class Practice.* With books still closed, model each line and have the whole class repeat in unison.
4. *Reading.* With books open, have students follow along as two students present the model.

   (At this point, ask students if they have any questions and check understanding of new vocabulary. You may also want to call students' attention to any related language or culture notes, which can be found in the Guide Book.)
5. *Pair Practice.* In pairs, have students practice the model conversation.
6. *Exercise Practice.* (optional) Have pairs of students simultaneously practice all the exercises.
7. *Exercise Presentations.* Call on pairs of students to present the exercises.

   (At this point, you may want to discuss any language or culture notes related to the exercises, as indicated in the Guide Book.)

"Now Present Your Own Conversations"

In these activities that follow the guided conversations at the end of each lesson, have pairs of students create and present original conversations based on the model. Encourage students to be inventive as they create their characters and situations. (You may want to assign this exercise as homework, having students prepare their original conversations, practice them the next day with another student, and then present them to the class.) In this way, students can review the previous day's lesson without actually having to repeat the specific exercises already covered.

Expansion

We encourage you to use the expansion activity for each lesson suggested in the Guide Book or a similar activity that provides students with free, spontaneous practice while synthesizing the content of the lesson.

Interchange

Have students practice the model using the same steps listed above for guided conversations. (You might want to eliminate the *Class Practice* step in the case of longer Interchange dialogs.) After practicing the model, have pairs of students create and present original conversations using the model dialog as a guide. Encourage students to be inventive and to use new vocabulary. (You may want to assign this exercise as homework, having students prepare their own conversations, practice them the next day with another student, and then present them to the class.) Students should present their conversations without referring to the written text, but they should also not memorize them. Rather, they should feel free to adapt and expand them any way they wish.

Scenes & Improvisations

Have students talk about the people and the situations, and then present role plays based on the scenes. Students may refer back to previous lessons as a resource, but they should not simply re-use specific conversations. (You may want to assign these exercises as written homework, having students prepare their conversations, practice them the next day with another student, and then present them to the class.)

Multi-Level Classes

Teachers of multi-level classes may wish to modify some of the teaching suggestions mentioned above. For example, teachers who have their students do simultaneous pair practice can have students at lower levels practice fewer exercises while students at higher levels practice more or all exercises. During this pair practice, the teacher can offer special help to students at lower levels and perhaps tell them which particular exercise they should prepare for presentation to the class.

For multi-level classes with an exceptionally wide range of ability levels, the *ExpressWays—Book 1 Guide Books* indicate for each lesson the corresponding page in *ExpressWays—Foundations* that covers the same topic at a lower level and the corresponding page in *ExpressWays—Book 2* that covers the same topic at a higher level.

In conclusion, we have attempted to offer students a communicative, meaningful, and lively way of practicing the vocabulary, grammar, and functions of English. While conveying to you the substance of our textbook, we hope that we have also conveyed the spirit: that learning to communicate in English can be genuinely interactive . . . truly relevant to our students' lives . . . and fun!

Steven J. Molinsky
Bill Bliss

Components of an ExpressWays Lesson

A **model conversation** offers initial practice with the functions and structures of the lesson.

In the **exercises**, students create conversations by placing new contexts, content, or characters into the model.

The **open-ended exercise** at the end of each lesson asks students to create and present original conversations based on the model.

Examples:

Exercise 1:

A. Excuse me. Does this train go to Brooklyn?
B. No, it doesn't. It goes to the Bronx.
A. Oh, I see. Tell me, which train goes to Brooklyn?
B. The "D" Train.
A. Thanks very much.

Exercise 2:

A. Excuse me. Does this plane go to San Francisco?
B. No, it doesn't. It goes to San Diego.
A. Oh, I see. Tell me, which plane goes to San Francisco?
B. Flight 64.
A. Thanks very much.

- **HOUSING**
- **SOCIAL COMMUNICATION**
- **PERSONAL INFORMATION**

- Present Tense: Review • WH-Questions
- Yes/No Questions • Two-Word Verbs
- Past Tense: Review • Can • Could
- Should • Object Pronouns
- Possessive Adjectives • Time Expressions

Hello. I'm Your Neighbor
Is There a Laundromat in the Neighborhood?
Can I Park My Car Here?
Can I Help You Take Out the Garbage?
Could You Lend Me a Hammer?
I Knocked on Your Door Several Times Last Week
Maybe You Should Call a Plumber
Do You Fix Kitchen Sinks?

- Asking for and Reporting Information • Greeting People
- Attracting Attention • Gratitude • Appreciation
- Checking and Indicating Understanding • Initiating a Topic

Hello. I'm Your Neighbor

A. Hello. I'm your neighbor. My name is Helen.

B. Hi. I'm Maria. Nice to meet you.

A. Nice meeting you, too. Tell me, where are you from?

B. Mexico. And you?

A. Greece.

1. 5B
   3C

2. History
   Biology

3. the 5th
   the 3rd

4. Chicago
   San Francisco

5. I have a broken leg.
   I have high blood pressure.

Now present your own conversations.

Is There a Laundromat in the Neighborhood?

A. Excuse me. I'm new here. Can I ask you a question?

B. Sure.

A. Is there a laundromat in the neighborhood?

B. Yes. There's a laundromat around the corner.

A. Around the corner?

B. Yes.

A. Thanks very much.

1.

2.

3.

4.

5.

Now present your own conversations.

Can I Park My Car Here?

A. Pardon me. Can I ask you a question?

B. Certainly.

A. Can I park my car here?

B. Yes, you can.

A. Thanks.

A. Pardon me. Can I ask you a question?

B. Certainly.

A. Can I use my fireplace?

B. No, you can't.

A. Oh, okay. Thanks.

1.

2.

3.

4.

5.

Now present your own conversations.

Can I Help You Take Out the Garbage?

take out the garbage

A. Can I help you take out the garbage?

B. No. That's okay. I can take it out myself.

A. Please. Let me help you.

B. Well, all right. If you don't mind.

A. No, not at all.

B. Thanks. I appreciate it.

pick up your things

A. Can I help you pick up your things?

B. No. That's okay. I can pick them up myself.

A. Please. Let me help you.

B. Well, all right. If you don't mind.

A. No, not at all.

B. Thanks. I appreciate it.

1. hang up your laundry

2. put away these chairs

3. carry those bags

4. cut down that tree

5. clean up this mess

Now present your own conversations.

101

Could You Lend Me a Hammer?

lend me a hammer

A. Could I ask you a favor?

B. Yes.

A. Could you lend me a hammer?

B. All right.

A. Are you sure?

B. Yes. I'd be happy to lend you a hammer.

A. Thanks. I appreciate it.

1. help me start my car

2. lend me some flour

3. help me with my shopping bags

4. take care of Billy for a few minutes

5. pick up my mail while I'm away

"COULD YOU LEND ME A HAMMER?"

Now present your own conversations.

I Knocked on Your Door Several Times Last Week

A. You know, I knocked on your door several times last week, but you weren't home.

B. No, I wasn't. I was in Detroit.

A. Oh. What did you do there?

B. I visited my daughter and her husband.

A. Oh. That's nice.

1. in New York / see a Broadway show / I called you . . .

2. in Washington, D.C. / visit my cousins / I came* by . . .

3. in Colorado / drive through the Rocky Mountains / I rang* your doorbell . . .

4. at my son's house / take care of my grandchildren / I stopped by . . .

5. in California / go to Disneyland / I knocked on your door . . .

"I KNOCKED ON YOUR DOOR SEVERAL TIMES LAST WEEK"

Now present your own conversations.

* come–came
ring–rang

Maybe You Should Call a Plumber

A. What are you doing?

B. I'm trying to fix my kitchen sink.

A. What's wrong with it?

B. It's leaking.

A. I see.   And you're trying to fix it yourself?

B. Yes.   But I'm having a lot of trouble.

A. You know, maybe you should call a plumber.

B. Hmm.   You're probably right.

1. call an electrician

2. call a carpenter

3. call the gas company

4. call the superintendent

5. call a plumber

Now present your own conversations.

INTERCHANGE
Do You Fix Kitchen Sinks?

A. Ace Plumbing Company.

B. Hello. Do you fix kitchen sinks?

A. Yes. What's the problem?

B. My kitchen sink is leaking.

A. I see. We can send a plumber at two o'clock this afternoon. Is that okay?

B. Two o'clock this afternoon? Yes, that's fine.

A. Okay. What's the name?

B. Eric Jensen.

A. Spell the last name, please.

B. J-E-N-S-E-N.

A. And the address?

B. 93 Cliff Street.

A. Phone number?

B. 972-3053.

A. All right. A plumber will be there at two o'clock this afternoon.

B. Thank you.

A. Beaut_____ _____ me I help you

B. Hello. Do you fix _____ _____s?

A. Yes. What's the problem?

B. I can't see_____ _____. It's_____.

A. I see. We can send a hair style at eight oclock A. Is that okay?

B. eight oclock ___? Yes, that's fine.

A. Okay. What's the name?

B. NGA NGUYEN.

A. Spell the last name, please.

B. N-G-U-Y-E-N.

A. And the address?

B. 958 Beechnut St.

A. Phone number?

B. 561-____.

A. All right. A hair style will be there at eight oclock AM.

B. Thank you.

Something in your home is broken. Call a plumber, a carpenter, or an electrician, using the model dialog above as a guide. Feel free to adapt and expand the model any way you wish.

CHAPTER 10 SUMMARY

Topic Vocabulary

Housing

apartment
balcony
basement
building
doorbell
fireplace
floor
front door
garbage
garbage bags
garden
laundry
mail
neighbor
superintendent

Community

bus stop
laundromat
mail
supermarket

Household Fixtures and Appliances

kitchen sink
light
oven
radiator
stove
toilet

Household Repairs

carpenter
electrician
gas company
plumber

Personal Information

address
last name
name
phone number

Family Members

cousin
daughter
grandchildren
husband
son

Grammar

Simple Present Tense: Review

am   I'm your neighbor.
is   My name **is** Helen.
are   Where **are** you from?

do   Which apartment **do** you live in?
does   What time **does** the mail come?

WH-Questions

What's your major?
Where are you from?
Why are you here?
Which apartment do you live in?

Yes/No Questions

Is there a laundromat in the neighborhood?

Do they pick up the garbage today?

Two-Word Verbs

clean up this mess – **clean** it **up**
cut down that tree – **cut** it **down**
hang up your laundry – **hang** it **up**
pick up your things – **pick** them **up**
put away those chairs – **put** them **away**
take out the garbage – **take** it **out**

Past Tense: Review

I **was** in Detroit.
I **wasn't.**
You **weren't** home.

I **visited** my daughter.

I **saw** a Broadway show.
I **drove** through the Rocky Mountains.
I **took** care of my grandchildren.
I **went** to Disneyland.

   come–came
I **came** by.

   ring–rang
I **rang** your doorbell.

Can

Can I park my car here?
   Yes, you **can.**
   No, you **can't.**

Can I help you take out the garbage?
I **can** take it out myself.

Could

Could I ask you a favor?

Should

Maybe you **should** call a plumber.

Object Pronouns

Could you lend **me** a hammer?
I'd be happy to lend **you** a hammer.

Possessive Adjectives

Could you help me start **my** car?
I'd be happy to help you start **your** car.

Time Expressions

We can send a plumber **at two o'clock this afternoon.**

Functions and Conversation Strategies in this chapter are listed in the Appendix, **page 193.**

• EMPLOYMENT/ON THE JOB

• Future: Will • Can • Could • May
• Two-Word Verbs • Time Expressions
• Past Tense • Present Continuous Tense
• Have to

Could You Please Hand Me a Screwdriver?
Could You Possibly Type This Letter?
Do You Want Me to Give Out the Paychecks?
I'm Not Busy Right Now. Do You Want Any Help?
I Apologize
I'm Sorry I Was Late for Work This Morning
May I Please Leave at 4:00 Today?
Could I Possibly Take the Day Off Tomorrow?

• Requests • Permission • Offering to Do Something
• Offering to Help • Apologizing • Obligation
• Checking and Indicating Understanding • Hesitating

Could You Please Hand Me a Screwdriver?

A. Could you please hand me a screwdriver?

B. A screwdriver?   Okay.

A. Thanks.

B. You're welcome.

1.

2.

3.

4.

5.

Now present your own conversations.

Could You Possibly Type This Letter?

A. Could you possibly type this letter?

B. I'm sorry, but I can't.   I have to finish this report for the boss.

A. Oh, okay.

B. Sorry.

A. That's all right.   I'll ask somebody else.

1. mail these packages this afternoon?

2. work overtime tomorrow?

3. help me load the truck?

4. give me a ride home?

5. take Mr. and Mrs. Brown's luggage to Room 418?

Now present your own conversations.

Do You Want Me to Give Out the Paychecks?

give out the paychecks?

A. Do you want me to give out the paychecks?

B. Yes. If you don't mind.

A. Not at all. I'll be happy to give them out.

B. Thanks. I really appreciate it.

1. hang up the new calendar?

2. put away these glasses?

3. sort the mail?

4. set up the meeting room?

5. bag these groceries?

Now present your own conversations.

I'm Not Busy Right Now. Do You Want Any Help?

clean up the stockroom

A. I'm not busy right now. Do you want any help?

B. I don't think so. I'm just cleaning up the stockroom.

A. I'll be glad to help you clean it up.

B. Well, okay. It's nice of you to offer.

A. My pleasure.

1. take out the trash

2. file some reports

3. fold these towels

4. take down this sign

5. put up these decorations

"I'M NOT BUSY RIGHT NOW. DO YOU WANT ANY HELP?"

Now present your own conversations.

I Apologize

You didn't **turn off the lights** after work yesterday.

Barbara

A. Barbara?

B. Yes?

A. You didn't turn off the lights after work yesterday.

B. I apologize. I promise I'll turn them off in the future.

You **left the copying machine on** last night.

Larry

A. Larry?

B. Yes?

A. You left* the copying machine on last night.

B. I apologize. I promise I won't leave it on again.

You didn't **put away your tools** yesterday.

Frank

1.

You **forgot to punch in** this morning.

Howard

2.

You **gave out the paychecks too late** today.

Ms. Powers

3.

You didn't **spell my name correctly** in this letter.

Mr. Hinkel

4.

You **forgot to make holes** in the doughnuts.

Henry

5.

"I APOLOGIZE"

Now present your own conversations.

* leave—left

I'm Sorry I Was Late for Work This Morning

He was late for work this morning.

A. I'm sorry I was late for work this morning.

B. That's all right.

A. The reason is that I missed the bus.

B. I understand. Don't worry about it.

I had a bad headache.

1. She didn't come to work yesterday.

I went out the back door and forgot about the lights.

2. He left the lights on last night.

I had a flat tire on the way to work.

3. She missed the meeting this morning.

I was in a hurry to leave because I had a dentist appointment.

4. He forgot to lock the cash register yesterday evening.

I didn't remember the instructions.

5. He broke* the ice cream machine.

"I'M SORRY I WAS LATE FOR WORK THIS MORNING"

Now present your own conversations.

* break–broke

May I Please Leave at 4:00 Today?

A. May I please leave at 4:00 today?

B. At 4:00?

A. Yes. Is that all right with you?

B. Hmm. Well . . . I guess so.

A. Thank you.

1.

2.

3.

4.

5.

Now present your own conversations.

INTERCHANGE
Could I Possibly Take the Day Off Tomorrow?

A. Excuse me, Mrs. Clark.

B. Yes?

A. Could I possibly take the day off tomorrow?

B. Hmm. I don't think so.

A. I see. Uh . . . the reason I asked is my husband is going into the hospital tomorrow for an operation.

B. Oh, I understand. Well, in that case, I suppose you can take the day off tomorrow.

A. Thank you very much.

A. Excuse me, (Mr./Mrs./Ms./Miss) _____.

B. Yes?

A. Could I possibly _don't work today_____?

B. Hmm. I don't think so.

A. I see. Uh . . . the reason I asked is _my sister leaves today for_
_my country_____.

B. Oh, I understand. Well, in that case, I suppose you can _take this day_
_____.

A. Thank you very much.

You're asking your employer for permission to do something. Create an original conversation using the model dialog above as a guide. Feel free to adapt and expand the model any way you wish.

Topic Vocabulary

Objects on the Job

box
calendar
cash register
copies
copying machine
cup
decorations
desk
glass
groceries
letter
lights
line
luggage
machine
mail
napkin
package
paycheck
report
screwdriver
sign
table
tools
towel
trash
truck
window

Job Procedures

bag *these groceries*
clean up *table 12*
come in *late*
file *some reports*
finish *this report*
fold *these towels*
get *napkins*
give out *the paychecks*
hand me *a screwdriver*
hang up *the calendar*
help me
leave *the copying machine* on
load *the truck*
lock *the cash register*
mail *these packages*
make *5 copies*
punch in
put away *these glasses*
put up *these decorations*
set up *the meeting room*
sort *the mail*
spell *my name*
take down *this sign*

take out *the trash*
take *the day* off
take *this package*
transfer *this call*
turn off *the lights*
type *this letter*

Places on the Job

back door
front entrance
meeting room
Room *418*
Shipping Department
stockroom
supply room
warehouse

Additional Employment Vocabulary

boss
day off
employer
instructions
late
meeting
overtime
vacation

Grammar

Future: Will

I'll ask somebody else.
I'll be happy to give them out.

I **won't** leave it on again.

Can

I suppose you **can** take the day off tomorrow.

I'm sorry, but I **can't**.

Could

Could you please hand me a screwdriver?
Could I possibly take the day off tomorrow?

May

May I please leave at 4:00?

Two-Word Verbs

clean up the stockroom – **clean** it **up**
give out the paychecks – **give** them **out**
hang up the calendar – **hang** it **up**
put away these glasses – **put** them **away**
put up these decorations – **put** them **up**
set up the meeting room – **set** it **up**
take down this sign – **take** it **down**
take out the trash – **take** it **out**

Time Expressions

You didn't turn off the lights
  last night.
  this morning.
  today.
  yesterday.

May I please leave **at 4:00 today**?
May I please take the day off **tomorrow**?
May I please come in late **tomorrow morning**?
May I please take **next Monday** off?
May I please take my vacation **in July**?

Past Tense

I'm sorry I **was** late.

You **didn't** turn off the lights.

break–broke
I **broke** the ice cream machine.

forget–forgot
You **forgot** to punch in this morning.

leave–left
You **left** the copying machine on last night.

Present Continuous Tense

I'm cleaning up the stockroom.

Have To

I **have to** finish this report.

Functions and Conversation Strategies in this chapter are listed in the Appendix, **pages 193–194.**

• Imperatives • Prepositions of Location
• Future: Will • Time Expressions
• Past Tense • WH-Questions • May
• Could • Want to • Possessive Adjectives
• Object Pronouns

Could You Please Tell Me How to Make a
Long Distance Call?
I Want to Make This a Collect Call, Please
May I Please Speak to Betty?
When Is the Next Bus to Buffalo?
Please Fasten Your Seat Belt!
I Want to Report an Emergency!

• Asking for and Reporting Information • Instructing
• Identifying • Requests • Checking and Indicating Understanding
• Asking for Repetition • Initiating Conversations

Could You Please Tell Me How to Make a Long Distance Call?

make a long distance call

A. Excuse me. Could you please tell me how to make a long distance call?

B. Sure. Dial "one." Dial the area code. Then, dial the local phone number. Have you got it?

A. I think so. Let me see. I dial "one." I dial the area code. And then I . . . hmm. Could you repeat the last step?

B. Yes. Dial the local phone number.

A. Okay. I understand. Thanks very much.

A. Excuse me. Could you please tell me how to _use This pay phone_ ?

B. Sure. _pick up The receiver_
   put The money in the coin slot.
   Then, _Dial The number._
   Have you got it?

A. I think so. Let me see. I _pick up The receiver_
   I _put The money in the coin slot_
   And then I . . . hmm. Could you repeat the last step?

B. Yes. _Dial The number._

A. Okay. I understand. Thanks very much.

• Pick up the receiver.
• Put the money in the coin slot.
• Dial the number.

• Dial "zero."
• Dial the area code and local phone number.
• Tell the operator it's a collect call and give your name.

1. use this pay phone

2. make a collect call

• Dial "zero."
• Dial the area code and local phone number.
• Tell the operator it's a person-to-person call and give the name of the person you're calling.

3. make a person-to-person call

"COULD YOU PLEASE TELL ME HOW TO MAKE A LONG DISTANCE CALL?"

Now present your own conversations.

I Want to Make This a Collect Call, Please

A. Operator.

B. I want to make this a collect call, please.

A. What's your name?

B. Edward Bratt.

A. Did you say Edward Pratt?

B. No. Edward Bratt.

A. All right. One moment, please.

1. make this a person-to-person call

2. make this a collect call

3. make this a person-to-person call

4. make this a person-to-person collect call to Rose Wilson

5. charge this to my home phone

Now present your own conversations.

May I Please Speak to Betty?

A. May I please speak to Betty?

B. I'm afraid she isn't here right now.

A. Oh, I see.   When will she be back?

B. She'll probably be back in an hour.   May I ask who's calling?

A. This is her friend Steve.

B. Do you want to leave a message?

A. Yes.   Please ask her to call me when she gets back.

B. All right.   I'll give her the message.

A. Thank you.

1.

2.

3.

4.

5.

Now present your own conversations.

When Is the Next Bus to Buffalo?

A. When is the next bus to Buffalo?

B. It's at 4:10.*

A. At 4:10?

B. Yes.

A. I'd like a round-trip ticket, please.

B. All right. That'll be twenty-four dollars and fifty cents ($24.50).

1.

2.

3.

4.

5.

Now present your own conversations:

* 4:10 = four ten   † 3:07 = three "oh" seven
2:37 = two thirty-seven   11:05 = eleven "oh" five
10:55 = ten fifty-five
6:25 = six twenty-five

Please Fasten Your Seat Belt!

A. Excuse me. Please fasten your seat belt!

B. I'm sorry. I didn't hear you. What did you say?

A. I said, "Please fasten your seat belt!"

B. Oh, okay.

1.

2.

3.

4.

5.

Now present your own conversations.

INTERCHANGE
I Want to Report an Emergency!

A car just hit a pedestrian.

∧ Diane Lockwood

on Washington Street between *Second and Third Avenue*

A. Police.

B. I want to report an emergency!

A. Yes.   Go ahead.

B. A car just hit* a pedestrian.

A. Where?

B. On Washington Street between Second and Third Avenue.

A. Did you say Second and Third Avenue?

B. Yes.   That's right.

A. What's your name?

B. Diane Lockwood.

A. All right.   We'll be there right away.

* hit–hit

A. Police.

B. I want to report an emergency!

A. Yes. Go ahead.

B. _____.

A. Where?

B. _____.

A. Did you say _____?

B. Yes. That's right.

A. What's your name?

B. _____.

A. All right. We'll be there right away.

> Somebody just robbed a grocery store.

Ken Johnson

1. at the corner of *Broadway and K Street*

> There's a bad accident on Main Street.

Susan Bishop

2. in front of *the Hilton Hotel*

> A man just had a heart attack.

Alan Rogers

3. in the parking lot on *Maple Street*

> Somebody just mugged a jogger in the park.

Clara Hopkins

4. near *the statue of Robert E. Lee*

You're reporting an emergency. Create an original conversation using the model dialog above as a guide. Feel free to adapt and expand the model any way you wish.

Topic Vocabulary

Telephone

area code
coin slot
collect call
home phone
local phone number
long distance call
message
number
operator
pay phone
person-to-person call
receiver

charge
dial

Transportation

boat
bus
flight
train

ticket
one-way ticket
round-trip ticket

cars
door
seat
seat belt
white line

fasten
lean
ride
smoke
stand

Emergencies

accident
emergency
heart attack
pedestrian

hit
mug
report
rob

Grammar

Imperatives

Dial "one."
Dial the area code.
Then, dial the local phone
    number.

Please fasten your seat belt!
Please don't smoke on the bus!

Prepositions of Location

Please don't lean **against** the
    doors!
At the corner of Broadway and
    K Street.
Please stand **behind** the white
    line.
Please don't ride **between** the
    cars.
Between Second and Third
    Avenue.
In the parking lot.
In front of the Hilton Hotel.
Near the statue.
Please don't smoke **on** the bus!
On Washington Street.
Please put your bag **under** the
    seat **in front of** you.

Future: Will

When **will** he   be back?
            she
            they

He**'ll**   be back in an hour.
She**'ll**
They**'ll**

Time Expressions

She'll be back **in an hour.**
                    in about an hour.
                    in 2 or 3 hours.
                    in a few hours.
                    in a few minutes.
                    in a little while.

It's **at** 4:10 (four ten).
It's **at** 3:07 (three "oh" seven).

Past Tense

hit–hit
A car just **hit** a pedestrian.

say–said
I **said**, "Please fasten your seat
    belt!"

Somebody just robb**ed** a grocery
    store.

WH-Questions

Who are you calling?
What's your name?

May

May I please speak to Betty?

Could

Could you please tell me how to
    make a long distance call?

Want To

I **want to** make this a collect call,
    please.

Possessive Adjectives

This is **her** friend Steve.
This is **his** brother, Harold.
This is **their** lawyer, Ms.
    Kramer.

Object Pronouns

Please ask **her**   to call **me.**
              him
              them

Functions and Conversation Strategies in this chapter are listed in the Appendix, **pages 200–201.**

SCENES & IMPROVISATIONS
Chapters 10, 11, 12

Who do you think these people are?
What do you think they're talking about?
Create conversations based on these scenes and act them out.

1. Hello. I'm your neighbor. my name is Brown.

2. Can I help you?

3. Hello. Do you sell kitchen sinks?

4. I have to go to a meeting. go to school.

5.

6.

7.

8.

- **Partitives** • **Would** • **Count/Non-Count Nouns**
  - **Imperatives** • **May** • **Adjectives**

Do We Need Anything from the Supermarket?
What Do You Want Me to Get?
I Want a Pound of Roast Beef
Your Change Is $2.75
I'd Like a Hamburger and an Order of French Fries
I'd Like the Chicken
Would You Like a Few More Meatballs?
Can You Tell Me the Recipe?

- Want–Desire • Complimenting • Requests
- Preference • Instructing • Persuading–Insisting
- Checking and Indicating Understanding • Hesitating

Do We Need Anything from the Supermarket?

A. Do we need anything from the supermarket?

B. Yes. We need a quart of milk.

A. A quart?

B. Yes.

A. Anything else?

B. No, I don't think so.

A. Okay. I'll get a quart of milk.

B. Thanks.

1.

a pound of apples

2.

a gallon of orange juice

3.

2 boxes of rice

4.

a dozen eggs

5.

2 jars of mayonnaise

Now present your own conversations.

What Do You Want Me to Get?

A. Could you do me a favor?

B. Sure. What is it?

A. We need a few things from the supermarket.

B. What do you want me to get?

A. A can of tuna fish, a loaf of white bread, and a head of lettuce.

B. A can of tuna fish, a loaf of white bread, and a head of lettuce. Anything else?

A. No. That's all. Thanks.

a can of tuna fish

a loaf of white bread

a head of lettuce

a dozen oranges

a pound of butter

a bunch of bananas

1.

a gallon of skim milk

a bottle of ketchup

a jar of mayonnaise

2.

a bag of potato chips

2 loaves of whole wheat bread

half a gallon of apple juice

3.

a pint of vanilla ice cream

half a dozen eggs

2 bunches of grapes

4.

a jar of peanut butter

a quart of chocolate milk

a box of chocolate chip cookies

5.

"WHAT DO YOU WANT ME TO GET?"

Now present your own conversations.

I Want a Pound of Roast Beef

a pound of roast beef

a dozen rolls

A. May I help you?

B. Yes, please. I want a pound of roast beef.

A. Anything else?

B. Yes. A dozen rolls.

A. All right. That's a pound of roast beef and a dozen rolls. Is that it?

B. Yes. That's it.

4 pieces of chicken

a pound of American cheese

1.

a pound of ground beef

2 lamb chops

2.

3 doughnuts

a loaf of whole wheat bread

3.

a pound of potato salad

half a pound of Swiss cheese

4.

2 dozen hot dogs

3 jars of mustard

5.

"I WANT A POUND OF ROAST BEEF"

Now present your own conversations.

Your Change is $2.75

A. That'll be seven twenty-five ($7.25).

B. Seven twenty-five?

A. Yes.

B. Here's ten ($10).

A. All right. Your change is two dollars and seventy-five cents ($2.75). Here you are.

B. Thank you.

A. Have a nice day.

1. $1.15 _one fifteen_

2. $3.57 _three fifty-seven_

3. $8.40 _eight forty_

4. $6.08 _Six_

5. $.02

Now present your own conversations.

I'd Like a Hamburger and an Order of French Fries

A. Welcome to Burger King. May I help you?

B. Yes. I'd like a hamburger and an order of french fries.

A. Do you want anything to drink with that?

B. Yes. I'll have a cup of coffee.

A. Okay. That's a hamburger, an order of french fries, and a cup of coffee. Is that for here or to go?

B. For here.

A. That comes to two dollars and ninety cents ($2.90), please.

B. Here you are.

A. And here's your change. Your food will be ready in a moment.

for here
$2.90

1. to go
$2.65

2. for here
$4.10

3. to go
$5.05

4. for here
$4.80

5. to go
$27.94

"I'D LIKE A HAMBURGER AND AN ORDER OF FRENCH FRIES"

Now present your own conversations.

I'd Like the Chicken

A. What would you like?

B. I'd like the chicken.

A. All right. And would you prefer rice or a baked potato with that?

B. I'd prefer a baked potato.

A. And would you like anything to drink?

B. Yes. Let me see . . . I'll have a glass of milk.

A. Okay. That's the chicken with a baked potato, and a glass of milk.

1. noodles or rice?

2. french fries or
   mashed potatoes?

3. spaghetti or rice?

4. rice or a baked potato?

5. noodles or baked
   beans?

Now present your own
conversations.

135

Would You Like a Few More Meatballs?

meatballs

A. Would you like a few more meatballs?

B. They're delicious . . . but no, thank you.

A. Oh, come on! Have a few more.

B. All right, But, please . . . not too many.

salad

A. Would you like a little more salad?

B. It's very good . . . but no, thank you.

A. Oh, come on! Have a little more.

B. All right. But, please . . . not too much.

1. mushrooms

2. ice cream

3. cake

4. cookies

5. pie

Now present your own conversations.

INTERCHANGE
Can You Tell Me the Recipe?

A. Your cake was delicious. Can you tell me the recipe?

B. Sure. First, mix together a cup of flour, a teaspoon of salt, and two tablespoons of water.

A. I see.

B. Then, add half a cup of sugar. Are you with me so far?

A. Yes. I'm following you.

B. Okay. Next, add two eggs.

A. Uh-húh.

B. And then, put the mixture into a baking pan and bake for one hour at 350 degrees. Have you got all that?

A. Yes, I've got it. Thanks.

A. Your _____ was delicious. Can you tell me the recipe?

B. Sure. First, _____.

A. I see.

B. Then, _____.
Are you with me so far?

A. Yes. I'm following you.

B. Okay. Next, _____.

A. Uh-húh.

B. And then, _____.
Have you got all that?

A. Yes, I've got it. Thanks.

You're a dinner guest at somebody's home. Compliment the host or hostess and ask for a recipe, using the model dialog above as a guide. Feel free to adapt and expand the model any way you wish.

Topic Vocabulary

Food Items

apple
banana
beans
  baked beans
  refried beans
beef
  ground beef
bread
  white bread
  whole wheat bread
butter
cake
cheese
  American cheese
  Swiss cheese
cheeseburger
chicken
coffee
cole slaw
cookies
  chocolate chip cookies
doughnut
egg
fish
flour
grapes
hamburger
hot dog
ice cream
  vanilla ice cream
juice
  apple juice
ketchup
lamb chop

lemonade
lettuce
mayonnaise
meatballs
meat loaf
milk
  chocolate milk
  skim milk
mushrooms
mustard
noodles
orange
orange juice
peanut butter
pie
potato
  baked potato
  french fries
  mashed potatoes
potato chips
potato salad
rice
roast beef
rolls
salad
salt
sandwich
  fish sandwich
  roast beef sandwich
shake
  chocolate shake
soda
  Coke
  orange soda
  Pepsi
spaghetti

sugar
taco
tea
  iced tea
tuna fish
water
wine

Food Units

bag
bottle
box
bunch
can
dozen
gallon
head
jar
loaf–loaves
piece
pint
pound
quart

half a cup
half a dozen
half a gallon
half a pound

tablespoon
teaspoon

container
cup
glass

order
piece

small
medium
large

Purchasing Food

change
for here
"special of the day"
to go

Describing Food

delicious
excellent
fantastic
very good

Recipes

add
bake
baking pan
350 degrees
mix together
mixture
recipe

Grammar

Partitives

a bag of potato chips
a box of rice
a bottle of ketchup
a bunch of bananas
a can of tuna fish
a container of cole slaw
a cup of coffee
a dozen eggs
a gallon of orange juice
a glass of milk
a head of lettuce
a jar of mayonnaise
a loaf of bread
an order of french fries
a piece of chicken
a pint of ice cream
a pound of apples
a quart of milk

half a dozen eggs

half a gallon of apple juice
half a pound of cheese

a cup of flour
a tablespoon of water
a teaspoon of salt

Would

What **would** you like?
Would you prefer rice or a
  baked potato?

I'd like the chicken.
I'd prefer a baked potato.

Count/Non-Count Nouns

Count
Would you like **a few** more
  meatballs?
Have **a few** more.

They're delicious.
Not **too many**.

Non-Count
Would you like **a little** more
  salad?
Have **a little** more.

It's very good.
Not **too much**.

Imperatives

Add half a cup of sugar.

May

May I help you?

Adjectives

They're **delicious**.

Functions and Conversation Strategies in this chapter are listed in the Appendix, **pages 195–196.**

• Adjectives • Comparatives • Superlatives
• Ordinal Numbers • Past Tense • Should
• Future: Going to • Have to
• Time Expressions • Imperatives
• This/That

I Don't Think We Can Afford It
Can You Show Me a Less Expensive One?
I Think We Should Stop at the Bank
I'd Like to Deposit This in My Savings Account
I'm Balancing the Checkbook
Why Are You Banging on the Vending Machine?
Did You Remember to Pay the Telephone Bill?
I Think There's a Mistake on My Electric Bill

• Remembering/Forgetting • Describing
• Agreement/Disagreement • Certainty/Uncertainty
• Advice—Suggestions • Checking and Indicating Understanding
• Initiating a Topic

I Don't Think We Can Afford It

refrigerator
large

sofa
comfortable

A. Which refrigerator do you like?

B. I like this one. It's very large.

A. I know. It's larger than that one, but it's also more expensive.

B. Hmm. You're right.

A. I don't think we can afford it.

B. I suppose not.

A. Which sofa do you like?

B. I like this one. It's very comfortable.

A. I know. It's more comfortable than that one, but it's also more expensive.

B. Hmm. You're right.

A. I don't think we can afford it.

B. I suppose not.

1. air conditioner
quiet

2. rug
attractive

3. crib
nice

4. stereo system
good*

5. computer
powerful

Now present your own
conversations.

* good–better

Can You Show Me a Less Expensive One?

a firm mattress
$300

a comfortable armchair
$450

A. May I help you?

B. Yes. I'm looking for a firm mattress.

A. Take a look at this one. It's the firmest mattress in the store.

B. How much is it?

A. Three hundred dollars ($300).

B. I see. Can you show me a less expensive one?

A. Certainly. I'll be happy to.

A. May I help you?

B. Yes. I'm looking for a comfortable armchair.

A. Take a look at this one. It's the most comfortable armchair in the store.

B. How much is it?

A. Four hundred and fifty dollars ($450).

B. I see. Can you show me a less expensive one?

A. Certainly. I'll be happy to.

1. a large kitchen table
$225

2. a lightweight typewriter
$185

3. a big bookcase
$540

4. a good* cassette player
$160

5. a powerful computer
$3,750

Now present your own conversations.

* good–best

I Think We Should Stop at the Bank

buy stamps at the post office
take the kids to the zoo tomorrow

A. You know . . . I think we should stop at the bank.

B. Why? Do we need cash?

A. Yes. Remember . . . We have to buy stamps at the post office, and we're going to take the kids to the zoo tomorrow.

B. You're right. I forgot. How much do you think we should get?

A. I think forty dollars ($40) will be enough.

B. I think so, too.

1. buy food for the
   weekend
   see a movie tonight

2. pay the baby-sitter
   go out for dinner
   tomorrow night

3. buy a birthday present
   for Uncle Bob
   drive to the beach
   tomorrow

4. get an anniversary gift
   for your parents
   visit my sister in New
   York on Sunday

5. get more dog food for
   Rover
   go skiing this weekend

Now present your own
conversations.

142

I'd Like to Deposit This in My Savings Account

A. I'd like to deposit this in my savings account.

B. All right. Please print your name on the deposit slip.

A. Oh. Did I forget to print my name on the deposit slip?

B. Yes, you did.

A. Sorry.

Now present your own conversations.

I'm Balancing the Checkbook

A. What are you doing?

B. I'm balancing the checkbook.

A. Oh. I forgot to tell you. I wrote a check to Dr. Anderson for Billy's examination.

B. Oh. Do you remember the amount?

A. Yes. Seventy-five dollars ($75).

B. Okay. Thanks.

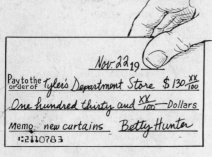

1.

2.

3.

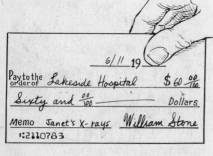

4.

5.

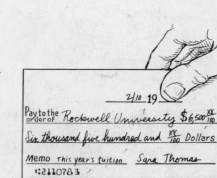

Now present your own conversations.

Why Are You Banging on the Vending Machine?

A. Why are you banging on the vending machine?

B. I'm trying to buy soda, but I just lost* my money.

A. What did you put* in?

B. A quarter and a dime.†

A. Thirty-five cents?   That's too bad! You should call the number on the machine and ask for your money back.

B. I will.

† a penny	a nickel	a dime	a quarter
1 cent	5 cents	10 cents	25 cents

1.

2.

3.

4.

5.

Now present your own conversations.

*   lose–lost
    put–put

Did You Remember to Pay the Telephone Bill?

A. Did you remember to pay the telephone bill?

B. The telephone bill? That isn't due yet.

A. Are you sure?

B. Yes. I'm positive. Look! Here's the bill. It's due on January 10th.*

A. Oh, okay.

*	January	(JAN)	July	(JUL)	1st – first	21st – twenty-first
	February	(FEB)	August	(AUG)	2nd – second	22nd – twenty-second
	March	(MAR)	September	(SEPT)	3rd – third	23rd – twenty-third
	April	(APR)	October	(OCT)	4th – fourth	24th – twenty-fourth
	May	(MAY)	November	(NOV)	5th – fifth	25th – twenty-fifth
	June	(JUN)	December	(DEC)	•	•
					•	•
					•	•
					20th – twentieth	30th – thirtieth

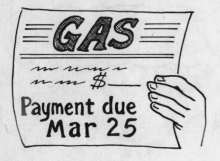

1.

2.

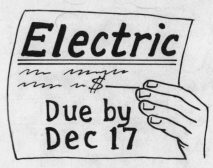

3.

4.

5.

Now present your own conversations.

146

INTERCHANGE
I Think There's a Mistake on My Electric Bill

A. Southeast Electric Company.   May I help you?

B. Yes.   I think there's a mistake on my electric bill.

A. Oh.   What's the problem?

B. I believe I was charged too much.

A. I see.   What is your name?

B. John Lawson.

A. And your account number?

B. 463 21 0978.

A. And what is the amount on your bill?

B. Four hundred and thirty dollars ($430).

A. All right.   Please hold and I'll check our records.

B. Thank you.

A. _____.   May I help you?

B. Yes.   I think there's a mistake on my _____ bill.

A. Oh.   What's the problem?

B. I believe I was charged too much.

A. I see.   What is your name?

B. _____.

A. And your account number?

B. _____.

A. And what is the amount on your bill?

B. _____.

A. All right.   Please hold and I'll check our records.

B. Thank you.

There is a mistake on one of your utility bills (electric, gas, telephone, oil, water, cable TV). Call the company and tell them about the mistake, using the model dialog above as a guide.   Feel free to adapt and expand the model any way you wish.

Topic Vocabulary

Furniture

armchair
bookcase
crib
kitchen table
mattress
rug
sofa

Department Store Items

cassette player
computer
stereo system
typewriter

Household Fixtures and Appliances

air conditioner
refrigerator

Describing

attractive
big

comfortable
expensive
firm
good
large
lightweight
nice
powerful
quiet

Finances

afford
balance
buy
pay

cash
check
checkbook
money

Banking

cash *this* check
deposit
endorse

make a withdrawal
print *your name*
sign *your name*

account number
amount
check
checking account
deposit slip
savings account
withdrawal slip

Coins

penny   – 1 cent
nickel – 5 cents
dime   – 10 cents
quarter – 25 cents

Utility Bills

cable TV bill
electric bill
gas bill
oil bill
telephone bill
water bill

account number
amount
due

Months of the Year

January (JAN)
February (FEB)
March (MAR)
April (APR)
May (MAY)
June (JUN)
July (JUL)
August (AUG)
September (SEPT)
October (OCT)
November (NOV)
December (DEC)

Grammar

Adjectives

It's very **large**.

I'm looking for a **firm** mattress.

Comparatives

It's **quieter** than that one.
It's **larger** than that one.

It's **more comfortable** than that one.

It's **better** than that one.

Superlatives

It's **the firmest** mattress in the store.
It's **the largest** kitchen table in the store.
It's **the biggest** bookcase in the store.

It's **the most comfortable** armchair in the store.

It's **the best** cassette player in the store.

Ordinal Numbers

1st – first
2nd – second
3rd – third
4th – fourth
5th – fifth
•   •
•   •
•   •
20th – twentieth
21st – twenty-first
22nd – twenty-second
23rd – twenty-third
24th – twenty-fourth
25th – twenty-fifth
•   •
•   •
•   •
30th – thirtieth

Past Tense

lose–lost
I just **lost** my money.

put–put
What did you **put** in?

Future: Going To

We're **going to** take the kids to the zoo tomorrow.

Should

You **should** ask for your money back.
I think we **should** stop at the bank.
How much do you think we **should** get?

Have To

We **have to** buy stamps.

Time Expressions

We're going to see a movie
on Sunday.
this weekend.
tomorrow.
tomorrow night.
tonight.

Imperatives

Please print your name.

This/That

I like **this** one.
It's larger than **that** one.

Functions and Conversation Strategies in this chapter are listed in the Appendix, **pages 196–197.**

• EMPLOYMENT/ON THE JOB

• Adjectives • Adverbs • Comparative of Adverbs
• Reflexive Pronouns • Past Tense • Imperatives
• Present Continuous Tense • Future: Will
• Time Expressions • Supposed to
• Have Got to • Might • Should
• Two-Word Verbs

Am I Assembling This Computer Correctly?
You Aren't Bagging the Groceries the Right Way
You're a Very Accurate Typist!
Am I Working Fast Enough?
Careful! Put On Your Safety Glasses!
Tony Is Hurt!
Will You Turn Off the Lights When You Leave?
May I Offer a Suggestion?

• Correcting • Approval/Disapproval • Obligation
• Warning • Advice–Suggestions • Complimenting
• Promising • Checking and Indicating Understanding
• Asking for Repetition

Am I Assembling This Computer Correctly?

attach the black wire to the switch on the back

Mr. Johnson

assemble this computer

A. Excuse me. Mr. Johnson?

B. Yes?

A. Am I assembling this computer correctly?

B. No, not exactly. You're supposed to attach the black wire to the switch on the back.

A. Oh, I see. Thank you.

put down the cover

Ms. Andrews

1. use the copying machine

list your hours on this line here

Tracy

2. fill out my timesheet

put the hamburger rolls next to the ketchup

Mr. Hobart

3. stock this shelf

put the forks on the left and the knives and spoons on the right

Mrs. Giovanni

4. set the tables

keep your chest out and your stomach in

Sergeant

5. stand "at attention"

"AM I ASSEMBLING THIS COMPUTER CORRECTLY?"

Now present your own conversations.

You Aren't Bagging the Groceries the Right Way

bag the groceries

A. Jimmy?

B. Yes?

A. You aren't bagging the groceries the right way.

B. I'm not?

A. No.   You've got to put the eggs on top.

B. Oh.   I didn't know that.   Thanks for telling me.

1. load the truck

2. transfer calls

3. operate the floor polishing machine

4. identify yourself to the guests

5. greet the customers

Now present your own conversations.

You're a Very Accurate Typist!

accurate typist

A. You're a very accurate typist!

B. Do you really think so?

A. Absolutely! You're typing very accurately.

B. Thank you for saying so.

1. careful painter

2. neat worker

3. fast* assembler

4. good* actor

5. effective speaker

Now present your own conversations.

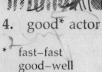
* fast–fast
good–well

152

Am I Working Fast Enough?

work fast

drive carefully

A. Am I working fast enough?

B. Actually, you should try to work faster.

A. Oh, okay. I'll try. Thanks for telling me.

A. Am I driving carefully enough?

B. Actually, you should try to drive more carefully.

A. Oh, okay. I'll try. Thanks for telling me.

1. give the instructions slowly

2. speak to the customers politely

3. make the sandwiches quickly

4. explain this grammar well*

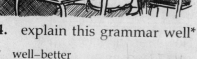

* well–better

5. sing loud

Now present your own conversations.

Careful! Put On Your Safety Glasses!

hurt yourself

A. Careful!

B. Excuse me?

A. Put on your safety glasses! You might hurt yourself.

B. Oh. Thanks for the warning.

1. fall down

2. start a fire

3. get hit by a car

4. get hurt

5. get a shock

Now present your own conversations.

Tony Is Hurt!

Tony burned himself on the stove.

A. Tony is hurt!

B. What happened?

A. He burned himself on the stove.

B. Tell him to put cold water on the burn. I'll get the first-aid kit.

A. Okay.

1. Carol fell* down a flight of stairs.

2. Charlie caught* his hand in his machine.

3. Sally cut* herself and she's bleeding VERY badly.

4. Mrs. Withers fainted and hit her head on the desk.

5. Leo got* hit by a forklift.

Now present your own conversations.

* fall–fell   cut–cut
catch–caught   get–got

Will You Turn Off the Lights When You Leave?

A. Will you turn off the lights when you leave?

B. Yes, I will.

A. Please don't forget.

B. Don't worry. I promise I'll turn them off.

1. clean up the supply room today

2. mail these packages this afternoon

3. pick up some pencils during your lunch hour

4. type this letter by 4 o'clock

5. put back these "Top Secret" files when you're finished

Now present your own conversations.

INTERCHANGE
May I Offer a Suggestion?

A. Excuse me, Mr. Mitchell.

B. Yes?

A. May I offer a suggestion?

B. Yes. Please.

A. I think we should put a juice machine with the other vending machines in the employee lounge.

B. I see. Why do you suggest that?

A. Well, it seems to me that many employees here don't like to drink coffee or soda.

B. Hmm. You might be right. Thanks for the suggestion. I'll think about it.

A. Excuse me, _____.

B. Yes?

A. May I offer a suggestion?

B. Yes. Please.

A. I think _____.

B. I see. Why do you suggest that?

A. Well, it seems to me that _____.

B. Hmm. You might be right. Thanks for the suggestion. I'll think about it.

Make a suggestion to your employer using the model dialog above as a guide. Feel free to adapt and expand the model any way you wish.

Topic Vocabulary

Occupations

actor
assembler
painter
typist
worker

Places on the Job

employee lounge
stairs
supply room

Objects on the Job

box
button
computer
copying machine
desk
files
first-aid kit
floor polishing machine
forklift
forks
fuse box
groceries
knives
letter
lights
machine
package
pencil
shelf
spoons
stove
switch
table
timesheet
truck
vending machine
wire

Job Procedures

assemble *this computer*
attach *the wire*
bag *the groceries*
clean up *the supply room*
drive
explain *this grammar*
fill out *my timesheet*
give *instructions*
go back and forth
greet *the customers*
hang up
identify yourself
knock *on the door*
list *your hours*
load *the truck*
mail *these packages*
make *the sandwiches*
operate *the floor polishing machine*
paint
pick up *some pencils*
press *the button*
put back *these files*
put down *the cover*
put *the hamburger rolls next to the ketchup*
say *"Room Service"*
set *the tables*
smile
speak to *the customers*
stock *this shelf*
transfer *calls*
turn off *the lights*
type *this letter*
use *the copying machine*
work

Feedback on Job Performance

accurate–accurately
careful–carefully
effective–effectively
fast–fast
good–well
loud–loud(ly)
neat–neatly
polite–politely
quick–quickly
slow–slowly

correctly
the right way

Job Safety

Caution
Danger
Do Not Touch
Helmets Required
High Voltage
No Smoking
Wait Here
Warning
Wet Floor

fire
safety glasses

Job Injuries

bleeding
burn *himself*
catch *his hand* in *his* machine
cut *herself*
faint
fall down
get a shock
get hit *by a car*
get hurt
hit *her* head
hurt *yourself*

Job Injury Procedures

Don't move *her.*
Get *her* some water.
Go back and stay with *him.*
Press on the cut.
Put cold water on the burn.
Turn off the power.

Call an ambulance.
Call the doctor.
Call the hospital.
Get *the school nurse.*

Additional Employment Vocabulary

customers
employees
employer
guests
hours
instructions
lunch hour
suggestion

Grammar

Adjectives

You're a very **accurate** typist!

Adverbs

You're typing very **accurately.**
      carefully.
      fast.
      well.

Am I working **fast** enough?

Comparative of Adverbs

You should try to work **slower.**
      faster.

You should try to work **more carefully.**
You should try to speak **more politely.**

You should try to work **better.**

Reflexive Pronouns

He burned **himself.**
She cut **herself.**

Past Tense

catch–caught
He **caught** his hand in his machine.

cut–cut
She **cut** herself.

fall–fell
She **fell** down a flight of stairs.

get–got
He **got** hit by a forklift.

Imperatives

Put on your safety glasses!
Don't smoke in here!

Tell him **to** put cold water on the burn.

Supposed To

You're **supposed to** attach the black wire to the switch.

Time Expressions

Will you mail these packages
  by 4 o'clock?
  during your lunch hour?
  this afternoon?
  today?
  when you leave?

Have Got To

You've **got to** put the eggs on top.

Might

You **might** hurt yourself.

Functions and Conversation Strategies in this chapter are listed in the Appendix, **page 197.**

SCENES & IMPROVISATIONS
Chapters 13, 14, 15

Who do you think these people are?
What do you think they're talking about?
Create conversations based on these scenes and act them out.

1. I wanted a pound of American cheese.

2. I'd like a hamburger and an order of French Fries to go.

3. I'd like the chicken, a baked potato and a glass of milk.

4. This suit is too long.

5. I'd like to Deposit This in My Saving account.

6. What are you doing? I'm balancing The checkbook

7. Can I help you?

8. Excuse me, you can't smoke in here.

• **GOVERNMENT AND LAW** • **DRIVING**
• **HOUSING** • **EMPLOYMENT/ON THE JOB**

• Impersonal Expressions with "You" • Past Tense
• Past Continuous Tense • Future: Going to
• Future: Will • Have to • Should • Ought to

Are You Allowed to Swim Here?
You Aren't Allowed to Park Here
"No Right Turn on Red"
Let Me See Your License
Rules of the Building
When Are You Going to Fix My Sink?
Do I Have to Work on July 4th?
You Should Write to the Mayor

• Permission • Asking for and Reporting Information
• Surprise–Disbelief • Promising • Focusing Attention
• Checking and Indicating Understanding • Initiating a Topic

Are You Allowed to Swim Here?

A. Are you allowed to swim here?

B. Yes, you are.

A. Thanks.

A. Are you allowed to smoke here?

B. No, you aren't.

A. Oh, okay. Thanks.

1.

2.

3.

4.

5.

Now present your own conversations.

You Aren't Allowed to Park Here

A. Excuse me. You aren't allowed to park here.

B. Oh?

A. Yes. There's the sign.

B. Hmm. "Parking for Handicapped Only." I didn't see the sign. Thanks for telling me.

A. You're welcome.

1. smoke

2. walk

3. stand

4. come in

5. eat

Now present your own conversations.

"No Right Turn on Red"

A. Oh, my goodness!*

B. What's the matter?

A. Didn't you see the sign?

B. The sign?   No.   What did it say?

A. "No Right Turn on Red."

B. "No Right Turn on Red"?!

A. Yes.

B. Oh, my goodness!*

1.

2.

3.

4.

5.

Now present your own conversations.

* Oh, my goodness!
  Oops!
  Uh-oh!

Let Me See Your License

A. Let me see your license.

B. Here you are, Officer. Tell me, what did I do wrong?

A. You went through a red light.

B. A red light?

A. Yes. I'm going to have to give you a ticket.

B. Oh.

1.

2.

3.

4.

5.

Now present your own conversations.

Rules of the Building

RULES OF THE BUILDING
- *Don't hang laundry on the balcony.*
- *Don't park in front of the entrance.*
- *Don't go on the roof.*
- *Don't leave garbage in the halls.*
- *Don't make noise after 11 p.m.*
- *Don't put things on the window ledges.*

hang your clothes there

A. Excuse me, but I don't think you're allowed to hang your clothes there.

B. Oh, really?

A. Yes. Tenants aren't permitted to hang laundry on the balcony. It's one of the rules of the building.

B. Oh. I didn't know that. Sorry.

A. That's okay.

1. leave your car here

2. put up that TV antenna

3. put your garbage there

4. play your stereo so loud at this hour

5. put flowerpots there

Now present your own conversations.

When Are You Going to Fix My Sink?

Mr. Grant in Apartment 2

A. Hello. This is Mr. Grant in Apartment 2.

B. Yes? What can I do for you?

A. I'm wondering . . . When are you going to fix my sink?

B. Well, Mr. Grant, I'm very busy right now. I'll try to fix it soon.

A. You know, you promised to fix it several weeks ago. I'm afraid I'm going to have to call the Health Department.

B. Now, Mr. Grant. I'm sure that won't be necessary. I promise I'll fix your sink this week.

A. Thank you very much.

repair our toilet

call the Housing Authority

1. Mrs. Lee in Apartment 9F

turn on our heat

call City Hall

2. Bill Franklin in Building 4

return our security deposit

go to court

3. Anita Davis, who lived in Apartment 6D

spray our apartment

call the Health Department

4. Ms. Fernandez at 659 Central Avenue

remove the lead paint in our kitchen

contact Channel 7 News

5. Mr. Dempsey on the fifth floor

"WHEN ARE YOU GOING TO FIX MY SINK?"

Now present your own conversations.

Do I Have to Work on July 4th?

A. May I ask you a question?

B. Sure. What is it?

A. Do I have to work on July 4th?

B. No, you don't. It's a legal holiday.

A. I see. Thank you.

1.

2.

3.

4.

5.

Now present your own conversations.

INTERCHANGE
You Should Write to the Mayor

A. You know . . . in my opinion, they should have more buses on this route in the morning.

B. Why do you say that?

A. The lines at the bus stops are long, the buses are too crowded, and people are often late for work.

B. Hmm. You should write to the mayor.*

A. Write to the mayor?

B. Yes. Really. You ought to write to the mayor and express your opinion.

A. That's a good idea. I will.

* **Some Forms of Citizen Participation**
  write to/call the President
  write to/call our congressman/congresswoman/senator
  write to/call the governor/mayor/city manager
  speak at a town meeting
  send a letter to the newspaper
  call a radio talk show

A. You know . . . in my opinion, _____.

B. Why do you say that?

A. _____, _____, and _____.

B. Hmm. You should _____.*

A. _____?

B. Yes. Really. You ought to _____ and express your opinion.

A. That's a good idea. I will.

You're talking with a friend about a local, national, or international issue. Create an original conversation using the model dialog above as a guide. Feel free to adapt and expand the model any way you wish.

Topic Vocabulary

Housing

apartment
balcony
building
entrance
garbage
hall
heat
kitchen
laundry
lead paint
noise
roof
rules
security deposit
tenant
TV antenna
window ledge

Recreation

camp
fish
ice skate
play ball
swim

Signs

Do Not Enter
Keep Off the Grass
No Fishing
No Food or Drinks
No Parking
No Smoking
No Standing in Front of the
    White Line
Parking for Handicapped Only

Road Signs

Do Not Enter
No Left Turn
No Right Turn on Red
No U Turn
One Way
Stop

Driving

illegal
license
90 miles per hour
Officer
red light
road
stop sign
ticket
U turn
wrong side of the road

drive
drive through *a stop sign*
go *90* miles per hour
go through *a red light*
make *an illegal U* turn
speed

Household Repairs

fix *my sink*
remove *the lead paint*
repair *our toilet*
spray *our apartment*
turn on *our heat*

Employee Rights

legal holiday
lunch break
maternity leave
overtime
radioactive
safety rules
union rules

Tenants' Rights

Channel 7 News
City Hall
court
Health Department
Housing Authority

Citizen Participation

call
express *your* opinion
send a letter
speak
write to

city manager
congressman
congresswoman
governor
mayor
President
senator

newspaper
radio talk show
town meeting

Grammar

Impersonal Expressions with "You"

Are **you** allowed to swim here?
    Yes, **you** are.
    No, **you** aren't.

You aren't allowed to park here.
I don't think **you're** allowed to
    hang your clothes there.

Past Tense

What **did** I do wrong?
    You **went** through a red light.

Past Continuous Tense

You **were** speeding.
You **were** driving on the wrong
    side of the road.

Future: Going To

When are you **going to** fix my
    sink?

I'm **going to** have to call the
    Health Department.

Future: Will

I'll try to fix it soon.
I promise **I'll** fix your sink this
    week.

I'm sure that **won't** be necessary.

Have To

Do I **have to** work on July 4th?

Should

They **should** have more buses
    on this route.
You **should** write to the mayor.

Ought To

You **ought to** write to the mayor.

Functions and Conversation Strategies in this chapter are listed in the Appendix, page 198.

• SOCIAL COMMUNICATION
• EMPLOYMENT/ON THE JOB

17

• Past Tense • Passive Voice • WH-Questions
• Simple Present Tense vs. To Be
• Future: Going to • Future: Will
• Might • Adjectives

I'm Sorry to Interrupt
What Does That Mean?
What's New with You?
Did You Hear the News?
I Like Your New Car
Did You See the "Phil Crosby Show" Last Night?
Did You Do Anything Special Over the Weekend?
What Are You Going to Do on Your Next Day Off?

• Asking for and Reporting Information • Complimenting
• Satisfaction/Dissatisfaction • Congratulating • Sympathizing
• Checking and Indicating Understanding • Initiating a Topic
• Interrupting • Clarification

I'm Sorry to Interrupt

A. Excuse me.   I'm sorry to interrupt, but we're out of fries.

B. Did you say pies?

A. No. Fries.

B. Oh, okay.   Thank you.

1.

2.

3.

4.

5.

Now present your own conversations.

What Does That Mean?

"They aren't working right now."

A. Our computers are down.

B. I'm afraid I'm not following you.   What does that mean?

A. What that means is they aren't working right now.

B. Oh.   I understand.

1. "There aren't any more seats on the plane."

2. "You're in excellent health."

3. "I'll pay for the dinner."

4. "He quit*."

5. "It's very popular."

Now present your own conversations.

* throw–threw
  quit–quit

What's New with You?

My son just got engaged.

I lost my wallet yesterday.

A. What's new with you?

B. Nothing much.   How about you?

A. I have some good news.

B. Really?   What?

A. My son just got engaged.

B. That's great!   Congratulations!

A. What's new with you?

B. Nothing much.   How about you?

A. I have some bad news.

B. Really?   What?

A. I lost my wallet yesterday.

B. That's too bad!   I'm sorry to hear that.

1. I just received a raise.

2. My husband got fired from his job.

3. I'm going to be promoted.

4. Our landlord is going to raise our rent again next month.

5. My daughter had a baby boy yesterday.

Now present your own conversations.

Did You Hear the News?

The boss is going to retire.

I heard it in the cafeteria.

A. Did you hear the news?

B. No. What?

A. The boss is going to retire.

B. Really? I can't believe it! Where did you hear that?

A. I heard it in the cafeteria.

B. Well, I'm really surprised.

They might lay off the workers on the night shift.

1. I heard it in the employee lounge.

Our supervisor had a big argument with the boss.

2. One of the secretaries told* me.

We might go on strike.

3. They talked about it at a union meeting.

The company is going to transfer Mr. Kendall to the West Coast office.

4. I overheard* it on the elevator.

The office manager and the receptionist got married last weekend.

5. Everybody in the office is talking about it.

Now present your own conversations.

* tell–told   overhear–overheard

175

I Like Your New Car

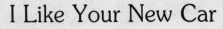

new car
fancy

A. I like your new car. It's very fancy.

B. Thank you.

A. How does it ride?

B. Very well.

1. engagement ring
   beautiful

2. jeans
   stylish

3. daughter
   friendly

4. haircut
   nice

5. new coat
   attractive

Now present your own conversations.

* buy–bought

176

Did You See the "Phil Crosby Show" Last Night?

the "Phil Crosby Show"?

funny?

A. Did you see the "Phil Crosby Show" last night?

B. No, I didn't.

A. You missed a really good one.

B. Oh? What happened?

A. Phil went to the zoo with his children and a monkey stole* his wallet.

B. Oh. Was it funny?

A. Yes. It was VERY funny.

B. I'm sorry I missed it.

Phil went to the zoo with his children and a monkey stole his wallet.

"City Hospital"?   dramatic?

1. Dr. Crane fell in love with one of his patients.

"60 Minutes"?   interesting?

2. They interviewed the President.

"Monica and Molly"?   funny?

3. Monica hit Molly's boyfriend with a lamp.

the Mets game?   exciting?

4. Hernandez hit five home runs.

the "Monster Movie"?   scary?

5. Green people from Mars attacked San Francisco.

"DID YOU SEE THE 'PHIL CROSBY SHOW' LAST NIGHT?"

Now present your own conversations.

* steal–stole

Did You Do Anything Special Over the Weekend?

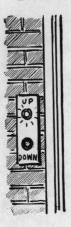

go to a rock concert

A. Did you do anything special over the weekend?

B. Yes. I went to a rock concert.

A. Oh. Who did you go with?

B. I went with my boyfriend.

A. Did you enjoy it?

B. Yes. We enjoyed it a lot.

1. go skiing with my family

2. see a movie

3. go to a ballgame

4. go to the Super Bowl

5. take my children to New York City

Now present your own conversations.

INTERCHANGE
What Are You Going to Do on Your Next Day Off?

A. What are you going to do on your next day off?

B. I'm not sure. I'll probably clean my apartment. How about you?

A. I don't know. I might go to a museum, or maybe I'll visit my parents. I'm not sure yet.

B. Well, whatever you decide to do, I hope you enjoy yourself.

A. Thanks. You, too.

A. What are you going to do _____?

B. I'm not sure. I'll probably _____. How about you?

A. I don't know. I might _____, or maybe I'll _____. I'm not sure yet.

B. Well, whatever you decide to do, I hope you enjoy yourself.

A. Thanks. You, too.

What are you going to do on your next day off?

What are you going to do on your next vacation?

What are you going to do this weekend?

What are you going to do over the holiday?

You and a co-worker are talking about your plans. Create an original conversation using the model dialog above as a guide. Feel free to adapt and expand the model any way you wish.

CHAPTER 17 SUMMARY

Topic Vocabulary

Places on the Job

cafeteria
elevator
employee lounge
fifth floor
Room *15*

Objects on the Job

nails
phone
screws

People on the Job

boss
co-worker
office manager
receptionist
secretary
supervisor
workers

Additional Employment Vocabulary

company
night shift
office
strike
union meeting

be promoted
get fired
lay off
quit
raise
retire
transfer

day off
holiday
vacation
weekend

Describing

attractive
beautiful
fancy
friendly
nice
stylish

dramatic
exciting
funny
interesting
scary

Recreation and Entertainment

ballgame
Broadway show
game
movie
mountain
museum
rock concert
show
Super Bowl
tickets

Grammar

Past Tense

Did you hear the news?
Where **did** you hear that?
No, I **didn't.**

Was it funny?
  It **was** very funny.

Dr. Crane **fell** in love.
My husband **got** fired from his job.
My daughter **had** a baby boy yesterday.
I **heard** it in the employee lounge.
Monica **hit** Molly's boyfriend.
I **lost** my wallet yesterday.
I **saw** "Star Battles."
Phil **went** to the zoo.

    buy–bought
I **bought** them at Sears.

    overhear–overheard
I **overheard** it on the elevator.

    quit–quit
He **quit.**

    steal–stole
A monkey **stole** his wallet.

    tell–told
One of the secretaries **told** me.

    throw–threw
Mr. Haskins **threw** in the towel
  today.

Passive Voice

My son just **got engaged.**
My husband **got fired** from his
  job.
I'm going to **be promoted.**

WH-Questions

Who cut it?
What is her name?
When did you get it?
Where did you buy them?
Why are you wearing it?
Which game did you see?
How does it ride?

Simple Present Tense vs. To Be

We need some more nails.
Tim Ross want**s** to see you.

Mrs. Hall **is** on the phone.
We're out of fries.
There's a broken window on the
  fifth floor.

Future: Will

I'**ll** probably clean my
  apartment.
Maybe I'**ll** visit my parents.

Future: Going To

I'm **going to** be promoted.
Our landlord is **going to** raise
  our rent.

What are you **going to** do on
  your next day off?

Might

I **might** go to a museum.
We **might** go on strike.
They **might** lay off the workers
  on the night shift.

Adjectives

It's very **fancy.**

Was it **funny?**
  It was very **funny.**

Functions and Conversation Strategies in this chapter are listed in the Appendix, pages 198–199.

• SOCIAL COMMUNICATION • EDUCATION • EMPLOYMENT/ON THE JOB

• Should • Short Answers • Pronoun Review
• Have Got to • Have to • Time Expressions
• Possessive Nouns

How Is David Doing in Math This Year?
This Is Mrs. Smith, the School Principal, Calling
I Agree
I Disagree
I've Really Got to Go Now
So Long
In My Opinion

• Agreement/Disagreement • Leave Taking • Obligation
• Asking for and Reporting Information • Initiating a Topic
• Focusing Attention

How Is David Doing in Math This Year?

Mrs. Carter
David

A. Hello. I'm Mrs. Carter.

B. Oh! David's mother! I'm pleased to meet you.

A. Nice to meet you, too. Tell me, how is David doing in Math this year?

B. He's doing very well. He works very hard, and his grades are excellent. You should be very proud of him.

A. I'm happy to hear that. Thank you.

1. Mr. Taylor
Judy

2. Mrs. Lee
George

3. Mr. and Mrs. Williams
Beth

4. Mrs. Mitchell
Tommy and Timmy

5. Mr. Atlas
Jack

Now present your own conversations.

This Is Mrs. Smith, the School Principal, Calling

A. Hello?

B. Hello. Is this Mr. Johnson?

A. Yes, it is.

B. This is Mrs. Smith, the school principal, calling.

A. Yes?

B. Michael started a fight in the school cafeteria this morning.

A. He did?

B. I'm afraid he did.

A. All right. I promise I'll speak to him about this when he gets home. Thank you for letting me know.

B. You're welcome. Good-bye.

Michael started a fight in the school cafeteria this morning.

Mr. Johnson

Mrs. Smith, the school principal

Wendy isn't doing her History homework.

Mrs. Thomas

Mr. Baker, Wendy's History teacher

1.

Richard didn't come for his eye test today.

Mrs. Lane

Miss Fenwick, the school nurse

2.

Patty is cutting classes every day.

Ms. Wilkins

Mr. Harris, Patty's guidance counselor

3.

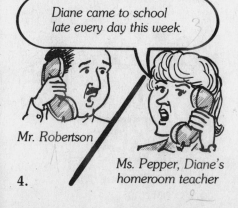

Diane came to school late every day this week.

Mr. Robertson

Ms. Pepper, Diane's homeroom teacher

4.

Henry won't take a shower after gym class.

Mr. Simmons

Coach Bradley

5.

"THIS IS MRS. SMITH, THE SCHOOL PRINCIPAL, CALLING"

Now present your own conversations.

I Agree

The boss is in a terrible mood today.

We probably shouldn't bother him.

A. You know . . . the boss is in a terrible mood today.

B. I agree.   He is.

A. We probably shouldn't bother him.

B. You're right.   I was thinking the same thing.

These copies don't look very good.

Maybe we should do them again.

1.

The soup is cold.

It doesn't taste very good.

2.

The mall was very quiet today.

Everybody was probably at the beach.

3.

Our English teacher taught us a lot.

We should have a party for her.

4.

It looks like a storm is coming.

We should probably close the pool.

5.

Now present your own conversations.

I Disagree

A. You know . . . I think this bread is stale.

B. Oh? Why do you say that?

A. It feels very hard. Don't you agree?

B. No, not really. I disagree.

1.

2.

3.

4.

5.

Now present your own conversations.

I've Really Got to Go Now

get back to work

A. By the way, what time is it?

B. It's 1:30.

A. Oh! It's late! I've really got to go now. I have to get back to work.

B. Okay. See you soon.

A. Good-bye.

1. pick up my kids at school

2. get to class

3. mail these letters before the post office closes

4. get to the bank by 4:00

5. be at the White House in ten minutes

Now present your own conversations.

So Long

pick up my wife at the office

A. You know, I think I should be going now. I've got to pick up my wife at the office.

B. I should be going, too.

A. So long.

B. See you soon.

1. be home before dark

2. buy some food for dinner

3. catch the 6:23 train

4. meet with my advisor in five minutes

5. get to my next performance

Now present your own conversations.

INTERCHANGE
In My Opinion

A. You know . . . I think English is an easy language to learn. Don't you agree?

B. Well, I'm not so sure. Why do you say that?

A. The grammar rules are very easy. Don't you think so?

B. No, not really. I disagree. In my opinion, English is a very difficult language.

A. Oh? What makes you say that?

B. You don't always pronounce English words the way you spell them.

A. Hmm. Maybe you're right.

A. You know . . . I think _____.
Don't you agree?

B. Well, I'm not so sure. Why do you say that?

A. _____. Don't you think so?

B. No, not really. I disagree. In my opinion, _____
_____.

A. Oh? What makes you say that?

B. _____.

A. Hmm. Maybe you're right.

You're having a disagreement with somebody. Create an original conversation using the model dialog on p. 188 as a guide. Feel free to adapt and expand the model any way you wish.

Topic Vocabulary

School Subjects

French
History
Math
Physical Education (gym class)
Science
Spelling

School Personnel

advisor
coach
guidance counselor
homeroom teacher
nurse
principal
teacher

Additional Education Vocabulary

cafeteria
class
eye test
grades
homework

Employment

boss
classified ads
copy
job
office
office assistant
supervisor

Grammar

Should

I think I **should** be going now.
Maybe we **should** do them
again.

We probably **shouldn't** bother
him.

Short Answers

It does.
They don't.
He is.
She is.
It is.
She isn't.
He did.
She did.
He didn't.
It was.
He won't.

Pronoun Review

He works very hard.
His grades are excellent.
You should be very proud of
him.

She works very hard.
Her grades are excellent.
You should be very proud of
her.

They work very hard.
Their grades are excellent.
You should be very proud of
them.

Have Got To

I've **got to** go now.
I've **got to** pick up my wife at
the office.

Have To

I **have to** get back to work.

Time Expressions

It's **3:00 (three o'clock).**
It's **1:30 (one thirty).**
It's **11:20 (eleven twenty).**
It's **4:45 (four forty-five).**

I have to mail these letters
before the post office closes.
by 4:00.
in ten **minutes.**

Possessive Nouns

/s/   Jack's father
/z/   David's mother
/ɪz/   George's mother

Functions and Conversation Strategies in this chapter are listed in the Appendix, **pages 199–200.**

SCENES & IMPROVISATIONS
Chapters 16, 17, 18

Who do you think these people are?
What do you think they're talking about?
Create conversations based on these scenes and act them out.

1. excuse me, you can't Fishing in here.

2. you drove Through a stop sign.

3.

4.

HOT DOG $1.00
B.L.T. $2.75

HAM & CHEESE
$3.25

CHEFS SALAD
$4.25

5.

6.

7.

8.

CHAPTER 10

Functions

Asking for and Reporting Information

Tell me, _____?

What's *your major?*
Where *are you from?*
Why *are you here?*
Which *apartment do you live in?*

And you?

Can I ask you a question?

Is there *a laundromat in the neighborhood?*
There's *a laundromat around the corner.*

I was in *Detroit.*
What did you do *there?*
I *visited my daughter and her husband.*

What are you doing?

What's wrong with *it?*
What's the problem?
It's *leaking.*

Do you *fix kitchen sinks?*

What's the name?
Eric Jensen.
Spell the last name, please.
J-E-N-S-E-N.
And the address?
93 Cliff Street.
Phone number?
972-3053.

Greeting People

Hello.
Hi.

Nice to meet you.
Nice meeting you, too.

Attracting Attention

Excuse me.
Pardon me.

Gratitude

Expressing . . .

Thank you.
Thanks.
Thanks very much.

Appreciation

I appreciate it.

Introductions

Introducing Oneself

I'm *your neighbor.*

My name is *Helen.*
I'm *Maria.*

Permission

Inquiring about Permissibility

Can I *park my car here?*

Indicating Permissibility

Yes, you can.

No, you can't.

Offering to Help

Making an Offer

Can I help you *take out the garbage?*

Let me help you.

Responding to an Offer

No. That's okay.

Well, all right.

If you don't mind.

Thanks. I appreciate it.

Persuading-Insisting

Please.

Requests

Direct, Polite

Could I ask you a favor?

Could you *lend me a hammer?*

Responding to Requests

All right.

I'd be happy to *lend you a hammer.*

Advice-Suggestions

Offering . . .

Maybe you should *call a plumber.*

Responding to . . .

You're probably right.

Identifying

Ace Plumbing Company.

Conversation Strategies

Checking and Indicating Understanding

Checking One's Own Understanding

Around the corner?
Two o'clock this afternoon?

Indicating Understanding

I see.

Initiating a Topic

You know, _____.

CHAPTER 11

Functions

Requests

Direct, More Polite

Could you please *hand me a screwdriver?*
Could you possibly *type this letter?*

Responding to Requests

Okay.

I'm sorry, but I can't.

Permission

Asking for . . .

193

May I please *leave at 4:00?*
Could I possibly *take the day off tomorrow?*

Is that all right with you?

Granting . . .

I guess so.
I suppose you can *take the day off tomorrow.*

Denying . . .

I don't think so.

Offering to Do Something

Making an Offer

Do you want me to *give out the paychecks?*

I'll be happy to *give them out.*

Responding to an Offer

Yes. If you don't mind.
Thanks.
I really appreciate it.

Offering to Help

Making an Offer

Do you want any help?

I'll be glad to help you *clean it up.*

Responding to an Offer

It's nice of you to offer.

Apologizing

Sorry.
I apologize.

I'm sorry *I was late.*
I'm sorry, but *I can't.*

Obligation

Expressing . . .

I have to *finish this report.*

Gratitude

Expressing . . .

Thank you.
Thanks.
Thank you very much.

It's nice of you to *offer.*

Responding to . . .

You're welcome.
My pleasure.

Ability/Inability

Expressing Inability

I can't.

Granting Forgiveness

That's all right.
I understand.
Don't worry about it.

Appreciation

I really appreciate it.

Attracting Attention

Barbara?
Excuse me, *Mrs. Clark.*

Remembering/Forgetting

Indicating . . .

I didn't remember *the instructions.*
I forgot about *the lights.*
I forgot to *lock the cash register.*

You forgot to *punch in.*

Promising

Offering a Promise

I promise *I'll turn them off.*
I promise *I won't leave it on again.*

Denying/Admitting

Admitting

The reason is that *I missed the bus.*

Conversation Strategies

Checking and Indicating Understanding

Checking One's Own Understanding

A screwdriver?
At 4:00?

Indicating Understanding

I see.
I understand.

Hesitating

Hmm.
Well . . .

CHAPTER 12

Functions

Asking for and Reporting Information

Could you please tell me *how to make a long distance call?*

May I ask *who's calling?*

What's your name?
Edward Bratt.

I'm afraid *she* isn't here right now.
When will *she* be back?
She'll probably be back *in an hour.*

When is the next *bus* to *Buffalo?*
It's at *4:10.*

That'll be *twenty-four dollars and fifty cents.*

I want to report an emergency!

A car just hit a pedestrian.

Instructing

Dial "one." Dial the area code. Then, dial the local phone number.

Identifying

Operator.
Police.

This is *her friend Steve.*

Requests

Direct, Polite

Please *fasten your seat belt.*

Please ask *her* to call *me.*

Responding to Requests

All right.
Oh, okay.

Attracting Attention

Excuse me.

Gratitude

Expressing . . .

Thanks very much.

Want-Desire

Inquiring about . . .

Do you want to *leave a message?*

Expressing . . .

I want to *make this a collect call*, please.

I'd like *a round-trip ticket*, please.

Correcting

Giving Correction

No. *Edward Bratt.*

Probability/Improbability

Expressing Probability

She'll probably *be back in an hour.*

Directions-Location

Inquiring about Location

Where?

Giving Location

At the corner of *Broadway and K Street.*
In front of *the Hilton Hotel.*
In *the parking lot* on *Maple Street.*
Near *the statue of Robert E. Lee.*
On *Washington Street* between *Second and Third Avenue.*

Conversation Strategies

Checking and Indicating Understanding

Checking Another Person's Understanding

Have you got it?

Checking One's Own Understanding

Let me see.

Did you say *Edward Pratt?*

At 4:10?

Indicating Understanding

Okay.
I understand.
Oh, I see.

Asking for Repetition

Could you repeat the last step?

I'm sorry. I didn't hear you. What did you say?

Initiating Conversations

May I please speak to *Betty?*

CHAPTER 13

Functions

Want-Desire

Inquiring about . . .

What would you like?

Would you like *anything to drink?*
Do you want *anything to drink?*

What do you want me to *get?*

Expressing . . .

I want *a pound of roast beef.*
I'd like *a hamburger.*
I'll have *a cup of coffee.*

We need *a few things from the supermarket.*

Complimenting

Expressing Compliments

It's/They're { delicious.
very good.
excellent.
fantastic.

Your *cake* was delicious.

Requests

Direct, Polite

Could you do me a favor?

Responding to Requests

Sure.

Preference

Inquiring about . . .

Would you prefer *rice* or *a baked potato?*

Expressing . . .

I'd prefer *a baked potato.*

Instructing

First, *mix together a cup of flour, a teaspoon of salt, and two tablespoons of water.*
Then, *add half a cup of sugar.*
Next, *add two eggs.*
And then, *put the mixture into a baking pan.*

Persuading-Insisting

Oh, come on!

Asking for and Reporting Information

Do we need *anything from the supermarket?*
Yes. We need *a quart of milk.*

That'll be *seven twenty-five.*
That comes to *two dollars and ninety cents.*

Your change is *two dollars and seventy-five cents.*

Can you tell me *the recipe?*

Intention

Expressing . . .

I'll *get a quart of milk.*

Gratitude

Thank you.
Thanks.

Offering to Help

Making an Offer

May I help you?

Leave Taking

Have a nice day.

Greeting People

Welcome to *Burger King.*

Conversation Strategies

Checking and Indicating Understanding

Checking Another Person's Understanding

Are you with me so far?

Have you got all that?

Checking One's Own Understanding

A quart?
Seven twenty-five?

A can of tuna fish, a loaf of white bread, and a head of lettuce.

That's a pound of roast beef and a dozen rolls.
Okay. That's a hamburger, an order of french fries, and a cup of coffee.

Indicating Understanding

I see.
Uh-húh.
I'm following you.
I've got it.

Hesitating

Let me see . . .

CHAPTER 14

Functions

Remembering/Forgetting

Inquiring about . . .

Did you remember to pay the telephone bill?

Do you remember the amount?

Did I forget to print my name on the deposit slip?

Indicating . . .

I forgot. quén
I forgot to tell you.

Reminding . . .

Remember . . . We have to buy stamps.

Describing

It's very large.

It's larger than that one.

It's the firmest mattress in the store.

Agreement/Disagreement

Expressing Agreement

I know.
You're right.
I think so, too.

I suppose not.

Certainty/Uncertainty

Inquiring about . . .

Are you sure?

Expressing Certainty

I'm positive.

I think there's a mistake on my electric bill.
I believe I was charged too much.

Advice-Suggestions

Asking for . . .

How much do you think we should get?

Offering . . .

I think we should stop at the bank.

I think forty dollars will be enough.

You should ask for your money back.

Preference

Inquiring about . . .

Which refrigerator do you like?

Expressing . . .

I like this one.

Offering to Help

Making an Offer

May I help you?

Want-Desire

Expressing . . .

I'm looking for a firm mattress.

I'd like to deposit this in my savings account.

Asking for and Reporting Information

How much is it?
Three hundred dollars.

Why are you banging on the vending machine?

What is your name?
John Lawson.
And your account number?
463 21 0978
And what is the amount on your bill?
Four hundred and thirty dollars.

Requests

Direct, Polite

Can you show me a less expensive one?

Please print your name on the deposit slip.

Responding to Requests

Certainly.

I'll be happy to.

Obligation

Expressing . . .

We have to buy stamps.

Intention

Expressing . . .

I will.

We're going to take the kids to the zoo tomorrow.

Apologizing

Sorry.

Gratitude

Expressing . . .

Thank you.
Thanks.

Sympathizing

That's too bad!

Identifying

Southeast Electric Company.

Conversation Strategies

Checking and Indicating Understanding

Checking One's Own Understanding

The telephone bill?

Indicating Understanding

I see.

Initiating a Topic

You know . . .

CHAPTER 15

Functions

Correcting

Giving Correction

You aren't *bagging the groceries* the right way.

You're supposed to *attach the black wire to the switch.*
You've got to *put the eggs on top.*

No, not exactly.

Responding to Correction

Oh, I see. Thank you.

Oh. I didn't know that.

Thanks for telling me.

Approval/Disapproval

Inquiring about . . .

Am I *assembling this computer* correctly?

Am I *working fast* enough?

Expressing Approval

You're *typing* very *accurately.*

Expressing Disapproval

Actually, you should try to *work faster.*

Obligation

Expressing . . .

You're supposed to *attach the black wire to the switch.*
You've got to *put the eggs on top.*

Warning

Be careful! cẩn thận, coi chừng
Careful!
Look out!
Watch it!
Watch out!

Put on your safety glasses!
Don't *stand there!*

Advice-Suggestions

Offering . . .

You should *try to work faster.*

I think *we should put a juice machine in the employee lounge.*

May I offer a suggestion?

Responding to . . .

Thanks for telling me.
Thanks for the suggestion.

I'll think about it.

Why do you suggest that?

Complimenting

Expressing Compliments

You're a very *accurate typist!*

Responding to Compliments

Thank you for saying so.

Do you really think so?

Promising

Offering a Promise

I promise *I'll turn them off.*

Attracting Attention

Excuse me. *Mr. Johnson?*
Excuse me, *Mr. Mitchell.*
Jimmy?

Possibility/Impossibility

Expressing Possibility

You might *hurt yourself.*

Gratitude

Expressing . . .

Thanks for *the warning.*

Asking for and Reporting Information

Tony is hurt!
  What happened?
He burned himself on the stove.

Instructing

Tell *him* to *put cold water on the burn.*

Intention

Expressing . . .

I'll *get the first-aid kit.*

Requests

Direct, Polite

Will you *turn off the lights when you leave?*

Responding to Requests

Yes, I will.

Remembering/Forgetting

Reminding

Please don't forget.

Agreement/Disagreement

Expressing Agreement

You might be right.

Conversation Strategies

Checking and Indicating Understanding

Checking One's Own Understanding

I'm not?

Asking for Repetition

Excuse me?

CHAPTER 16

Functions

Permission

Inquiring about Permissibility

Are you allowed to *swim here?*

Indicating Permissibility

Yes, you are.
No, you aren't.

You aren't allowed to *park here.*
I don't think you're allowed to *hang your clothes there.*
Tenants aren't permitted to *hang laundry on the balcony.*

Asking for and Reporting Information

May I ask you a question?

Tell me, _____?

What's the matter?

What did I do wrong?
   You *went through a red light.*

What did the sign say?

Why do you say that?

It's a legal holiday.

Surprise-Disbelief

Oh, my goodness!
Oops!
Uh-oh!

"No Right Turn on Red"?!
A red light?

Promising

Offering a Promise

I promise I'll *fix your sink this week.*

Attracting Attention

Excuse me.
Excuse me, but *I don't think you're allowed to hang your clothes there.*

Gratitude

Expressing . . .

Thank you.
Thank you very much.
Thanks for *telling me.*

Responding to . . .

You're welcome.

Apologizing

Sorry.

Granting Forgiveness

That's okay.

Identifying

Hello. This is *Mr. Grant* in *Apartment 2.*

Intention

Inquiring about . . .

When are you going to *fix my sink?*

Expressing . . .

I'll *try to fix it soon.*

I will.

Obligation

Inquiring about . . .

Do I have to *work on July 4th?*

Advice-Suggestions

Offering . . .

You should *write to the mayor.*
You ought to *write to the mayor.*

Responding to . . .

That's a good idea.

Conversation Strategies

Focusing Attention

You know, *you promised to fix it several weeks ago.*

In my opinion, *they should have more buses on this route.*

Checking and Indicating Understanding

Checking One's Own Understanding

Write to the mayor?

Indicating Understanding

I see.

Initiating a Topic

You know . . .

CHAPTER 17

Functions

Asking for and Reporting Information

What's new with you?
   Nothing much. How about you?

I have some good news.
I have some bad news.
   Really? What?

Did you see *the "Phil Crosby Show" last night?*
Did you *do anything special over the weekend?*

What happened?

Where did you hear that?
   I heard it *in the cafeteria.*
   One of the secretaries told me.
   They talked about it *at a union meeting.*
   I overhead it *on the elevator.*
   Everybody *in the office* is talking about it.

Who *cut it?*
What *is her name?*
When *did you get it?*
Where *did you buy them?*
Why *are you wearing it?*
Which *game did you see?*
How *does it ride?*

Complimenting

Expressing Compliments

I like *your new car.*

It's very *fancy.*

Responding to Compliments

Thank you.

Satisfaction/Dissatisfaction

Inquiring about . . .

Did you enjoy it?

Expressing Satisfaction

We enjoyed it a lot.

Congratulating

That's great!
Congratulations!

Sympathizing

That's too bad!
I'm sorry to hear that.

Correcting

Giving Correction

No. *Fries.*

Gratitude

Expressing . . .

Thank you.
Thanks.

Surprise-Disbelief

Really?

I can't believe it!
I'm really surprised.

Likes/Dislikes

Expressing Likes

I like *your new car.*

Describing

It was very *funny.*

Regret

I'm sorry *I missed it.*

Intention

Inquiring about . . .

What are you going to do *on your next day off?*

Certainty/Uncertainty

Expressing Uncertainty

I'm not sure.
I don't know.

I'm not sure yet.

Probability/Improbability

Expressing Probability

I'll probably *clean my apartment.*

Possibility/Impossibility

Expressing Possibility

I might *go to a museum.*
Maybe I'll *visit my parents.*

Wish-Hope

I hope *you enjoy yourself.*

Conversation Strategies

Checking and Indicating Understanding

Checking One's Own Understanding

Did you say *pies?*

Indicating Understanding

Oh. I understand.

Initiating a Topic

What's new with you?

Did you hear the news?

Interrupting

Excuse me.

I'm sorry to interrupt, but *we're out of fries.*

Clarification

Asking for Clarification

I'm afraid I'm not following you.
What does that mean?

Giving Clarification

What that means is *they aren't working right now.*

CHAPTER 18

Functions

Agreement/Disagreement

Inquiring about . . .

Don't you agree?
Don't you think so?

Expressing Agreement

I agree.
You're right.

Maybe you're right.

I was thinking the same thing.

Expressing Disagreement

I disagree.
I'm not so sure.

Leave Taking

I've really got to go now.

I think I should be going now.
I should be going, too.

Good-bye.
Bye.
Bye-bye.

So long.
See you soon.
Take it easy.
Take care.

I'll call you soon.

Obligation

Expressing . . .

I've got to *go now.*
I have to *get back to work.*

Asking for and Reporting Information

Tell me, _____?

How is *David doing in Math this year?*

Michael started a fight in the school cafeteria this morning.

I think *this bread is stale.*

Why do you say that?
What makes you say that?

What time is it?
It's *1:30.*

Introductions

Introducing Oneself

Hello. I'm *Mrs. Carter.*

Greeting People

I'm pleased to meet you.
  Nice to meet you, too.

Hello. Is this *Mr. Johnson*?

Approval/Disapproval

Expressing Approval

He's doing very well.
He works very *hard*.
His grades are excellent.

You should be very proud of *him*.

Gratitude

Expressing . . .

Thank you.
Thank you for *letting me know*.

Responding to . . .

You're welcome.

Identifying

This is *Mrs. Smith, the school principal*, calling.

Surprise-Disbelief

Oh!

He did?

It's late!

Promising

Offering a Promise

I promise I'll *speak to him*.

Advice-Suggestions

Offering . . .

We should *have a party for her*.
We should probably *close the pool*.
Maybe we should *do them again*.

We probably shouldn't *bother him*.

Conversation Strategies

Initiating a Topic

You know . . . *the boss is in a terrible mood today*.

Focusing Attention

In my opinion, *English is a very difficult language*.

TOPIC VOCABULARY GLOSSARY

The number after each word indicates the page where the word first appears.

(n) = noun
(v) = verb

Banking

account number 143
amount 143
cash *this* check 143
check (n) 143
checking account 143
deposit (v) 143
deposit slip 143
endorse 143
make a withdrawal 143
print *your name* 143
savings account 143
sign *your name* 143
withdrawal slip 143

Citizen Participation

call (v) 169
city manager 169
congressman 169
congresswoman 169
express *your* opinion 169
governor 169
mayor 169
newspaper 169
President 169
radio talk show 169
senator 169
send a letter 169
speak 169
town meeting 169
write to 169

Coins

penny – 1 cent 145
nickel – 5 cents 145
dime – 10 cents 145
quarter – 25 cents 145

Community

bank 142
bus stop 99
department store 144
hospital 115
laundromat 99
mail 99
mall 184
pharmacy 144
post office 142
supermarket 99
university 144
zoo 142

Department Store

cassette player 141
computer 140
stereo system 140
typewriter 141

Describing

attractive 140
beautiful 176
big 141
comfortable 140
delicious 136
dramatic 177
excellent 136
exciting 177
expensive 140
fancy 176
fantastic 136
firm 141
friendly 176
funny 177
good 140
interesting 177
large 140
lightweight 141
nice 140
powerful 140
quiet 140
scary 177
stylish 176
very good 136

Driving

Do Not Enter 164
drive (v) 165
drive through *a stop sign* 165
go *90 miles per hour* 165
go through *a red light* 165
illegal 165
license 165
make *an illegal U* turn 165
90 miles per hour 165
No Left Turn 164
No Right Turn on Red 164
No U Turn 164
Officer 165
One Way 164
red light 165
road 165
speed (v) 165
Stop 164
stop sign 165
ticket 165
U turn 165
wrong side of the road 165

Education

advisor 187
cafeteria 183
class 183
coach 183
eye test 183
French 182
grades 182
guidance counselor 183
History 182
homeroom teacher 183
homework 183
Math 182
nurse 183
Physical Education (gym class) 182
principal 183
Science 182
Spelling 182
teacher 183
tuition 144

Emergencies

accident 125
ambulance 155
emergency 124
heart attack 125
hit 124
hospital 155
mug 125
pedestrian 124
report (v) 124
rob 125

Employment

Employee Rights

legal holiday 168
lunch break 168
maternity leave 168
overtime 168
radioactive 168
safety rules 168
union rules 168

Feedback on Job Performance

accurate–accurately 152
careful–carefully 152
effective–effectively 152
fast–fast 152
good–well 152
loud–loud(ly) 153
neat–neatly 152
polite–politely 153
quick–quickly 153
slow–slowly 153
correctly 150
the right way 151

Job Injuries

bleeding 155
burn *himself* 155
catch *his hand* in *his machine* 155
cut *herself* 155
faint 155
fall down 154
get a shock 154
get hit *by a car* 154
get hurt 154
hit *her* head 155
hurt *yourself* 154

Job Injury Procedures

Call an ambulance. 155
Call the doctor. 155
Call the hospital. 155
Don't move her. 155
Get *her* some water. 155
Get *the school* nurse. 155
Go back and stay with *him*. 155
Press on the cut. 155
Put cold water on the burn. 155
Turn off the power. 155

Job Procedures & Skills

assemble *this computer* 150
attach *the wire* 150
bag *these groceries* 110
clean up *table 12* 108
come in *late* 114
drive 153
explain *this grammar* 153
file *some reports* 111
fill out *my timesheet* 150
finish *this report* 109
fold *these towels* 111
get *napkins* 108
give *instructions* 153
give out *the paychecks* 110
go back and forth 151
greet *the customers* 151
hand me *a screwdriver* 108
hang up 110
help me 108
identify yourself 151
knock *on the door* 151
leave *the copying machine* on 112
list *your hours* 150
load *the truck* 109
lock *the cash register* 113
mail *these packages* 109
make *five copies* 108
make *the sandwiches* 153
operate *the floor polishing machine* 151
paint 152
pick up *some pencils* 156
press *the button* 151
punch in 112
put *the hamburger rolls next to the ketchup* 150
put away *these glasses* 110
put back *these files* 156
put down *the cover* 150
put up *these decorations* 111
say *"Room Service"* 151
set *the tables* 150

201

IRREGULAR VERBS

be	was/were	lose	lost
bleed	bled	make	made
break	broke	mean	meant
buy	bought	meet	met
catch	caught	overhear	overheard
come	came	pay	paid
cut	cut	put	put
do	did	quit	quit
drive	drove	read	read
eat	ate	ride	rode
fall	fell	ring	rang
feed	fed	run	ran
feel	felt	say	said
find	found	see	saw
fit	fit	send	sent
forget	forgot	set	set
get	got	sit	sat
give	gave	speak	spoke
go	went	stand	stood
hang	hung	steal	stole
have	had	sweep	swept
hear	heard	swim	swam
hit	hit	take	took
hold	held	teach	taught
hurt	hurt	tell	told
keep	kept	think	thought
know	knew	throw	threw
lay	laid	understand	understood
leave	left	wear	wore
lend	lent	write	wrote
lie	lay		

INDEX OF FUNCTIONS AND CONVERSATION STRATEGIES

INDEX OF TOPICS

INDEX OF GRAMMATICAL STRUCTURES